# Instructions to the Regular and Rese... in case of an Air Raid.

For the purpose of looking after the interests of the public in case of a Raid by land or air, the Borough has been divided into twenty seven districts, viz.:—Seven each in the Southend, Westcliff and Leigh Sections, and two each in the Prittlewell, Southchurch and Thorpe Bay Sections. Each Reserve Section will be under the command of its Reserve Inspector, who will place a Sergeant in charge of each district in his Section. The Sergeant should have a first and second Officer to take his place in case of absence, who might be styled, Corporal and Lance-Corporal respectively.

Arrangements are to be made in each district for a parade point at which the men will meet in case of a raid. The Officer in charge will then distribute his men over the district under his control.

The first indication of a raid might possibly be received through the explosion of a bomb, or it may be that the Chief Constable would receive warning from the Military Authorities that hostile aircraft is in the vicinity. In the former case the Inspectors will instruct their men to assemble with all speed at the points arranged in the different Sections. In the latter case news would be sent through the regular Police to the Reserve inspectors.

Regular Police on duty will keep to their beats. Those off duty will assemble in uniform as quickly as possible at their respective Stations. The regulars of Prittlewell, Southchurch and Thorpe Bay will assemble at their parading points, and, in the absence of a superior Officer, be distributed over their districts by the senior Constable.

The men who parade at the Police Stations will be posted to beats by the Officer in charge, but at least three men will be kept in reserve at each Station.

Reserve Police should make themselves acquainted with the houses in their Sections where there are Telephones, and also with the Fire Alarm Boxes.

Both Regular and Reserve Police may at once begin to advise the public that unexploded bombs should not be touched, but information of such at once sent to the Police or Military Authorities.

A list is being prepared, and will be published later, of the names and addresses of persons available and ready with tools and appliances for the removal of fallen timber and debris.

Those Reserve Police who are members of the Ambulance and Voluntary Aid Brigades would work with these bodies in case of an air raid.

The duties of the Police in case of an air Raid will be:—

1. Prevent people gathering together in crowds.
2. Urge people to seek shelter at once.
3. Attend to injured until the First Aid Detachment arrive.
4. Call Fire Brigade if required and render assistance by keeping the way clear for the Firemen to work without hindrance.
5. In case the opportunity should arise, to see that no looting takes place.
6. If necessary to assist in releasing horses from vehicles.

## AMBULANCE AND VOLUNTARY AID DETACHMENTS.

Centres where Stretchers and Appliances are in readiness are at—
Ship Hotel, Marine Parade. Telephone No. 181.
Central Police Station. Telephone No. 81.
Feast and Osborne's Garage, Leigh Road. Telephone No. 51y1.
Fire Station, Leigh. Telephone No. 27.
Glen Hospital, Southchurch Road. Telephone No. 077.
Queen Mary's Hospital. Telephone No. 186.
Drill Hall, Prittlewell.—Prittlewell Railway Station. Telephone No. 230.

HOSPITALS.—The Glen Hospital, Southchurch Road;
The Victoria Hospital, Warrior Square;
The Overcliff (Hotel) Hospital, The Leas;
Queen Mary's Hospital;
will receive as many injured as can be accommodated and attend to out-door cases.

TELEPHONE NUMBERS.—Fire Brigade Stations—Southend, 90; Leigh, 27.
Police—Southend, 81; Westcliff, 41; Leigh, 28.

H. M. KERSLAKE,
*Chief Constable.*

FRANCIS & SONS, PRINTERS, SOUTHEND.

# A HISTORY OF
# SOUTHEND

Southend Pier, *c.*1905

# A HISTORY OF
# SOUTHEND

## Ian Yearsley

Phillimore

2001
Reprinted 2005


Published by
PHILLIMORE & CO. LTD
Shopwyke Manor Barn, Chichester, West Sussex

ISBN 1 86077 188 2

Printed and bound in Great Britain by
THE CROMWELL PRESS LTD
Trowbridge, Wiltshire

*This book*
*is dedicated to*
## my wife Alison,
*who was born in Southend,*
*and without whom it would not have been possible to finish it.*
*Thank you for all the time and effort you put in to help me.*

*Also to*
## 'The Guys' –
*Martin Crisp, Nigel Patel, John Spencer, Stuart Steele, Neil Stone and Simon Wingrove –*
*in memory of all the wonderful times we have spent together*
*in Old, New and modern Southend.*

# Contents

List of Illustrations . . . . . . . . . . . . . . . . . . . . . . . . . . . . . . . . .  ix

Acknowledgements . . . . . . . . . . . . . . . . . . . . . . . . . . . . .  xi


1.  Early History . . . . . . . . . . . . . . . . . . . . . . . . . . . . . . . .   1

2.  Prittlewell . . . . . . . . . . . . . . . . . . . . . . . . . . . . . . . .   7

3.  The 'South End' . . . . . . . . . . . . . . . . . . . . . . . . . . .  22

4.  Expansion . . . . . . . . . . . . . . . . . . . . . . . . . . . . . . . .  35

5.  The Town Council . . . . . . . . . . . . . . . . . . . . . . . . .  51

6.  From One War to the Next . . . . . . . . . . . . . . . . . . . . .  78

7.  Post-War Heyday and Major Change . . . . . . . . . . . . . . .  111

8.  Modern Times . . . . . . . . . . . . . . . . . . . . . . . . . . . . . .  130


Select Bibliography . . . . . . . . . . . . . . . . . . . . . . . . . .  142

Index . . . . . . . . . . . . . . . . . . . . . . . . . . . . . . . . . . . . . . .  145

# List of Illustrations

*Frontispiece:* Southend Pier, *c.*1905

1. Stone-Age finds . . . . . . . . . . . . . . . . . . . . . 1
2. Bronze-Age finds . . . . . . . . . . . . . . . . . . 2
3. Fossetts Farm hill-fort . . . . . . . . . . . . . . . . 3
4. Possible Late Bronze-Age camp off
   Eastern Avenue . . . . . . . . . . . . . . . . . . . 3
5. Iron-Age earthworks at Shoeburyness . . . . . . 4
6. Roman pottery . . . . . . . . . . . . . . . . . . . . . 5
7. Workmen in the Saxon cemetery at
   Prittlewell, 1923 . . . . . . . . . . . . . . . . . . . . 5
8. Saxon pendants . . . . . . . . . . . . . . . . . . . . . 6
9. Saxon arch at Prittlewell church . . . . . . . . . . 6
10. Prittlewell church . . . . . . . . . . . . . . . . . . . . 7
11. Model of Prittlewell Priory . . . . . . . . . . . . . . 8
12. Prittlewell Priory, showing foundations . . . . . 9
13. East Street, Prittlewell, *c.*1908 . . . . . . . . . . 11
14. North Street, Prittlewell, *c.*1913 . . . . . . . . 11
15. Prittlewell water pump, 1908 . . . . . . . . . . . 12
16. Chapman & André's map
    of Prittlewell, 1777 . . . . . . . . . . . . . . 13
17. Entrance to Priors Hall (Priory Park) . . . . . 14
18. Earls Hall, *c.*1900 . . . . . . . . . . . . . . . . . 15
19. Nazareth House (site of Milton Hall) . . . . . 16
20. Chalkwell Hall, *c.*1875 . . . . . . . . . . . . . . 17
21. The Crowstone . . . . . . . . . . . . . . . . . . . . 17
22. Porters . . . . . . . . . . . . . . . . . . . . . . . . . 18
23. Prittlewell village, showing medieval
    building, *c.*1900 . . . . . . . . . . . . . . . . . . 20
24. Deeds Cottage, 1945 . . . . . . . . . . . . . . . . 21
25. Old Southend Road . . . . . . . . . . . . . . . . . 22
26. Chapman & André's map
    of Southend, 1777 . . . . . . . . . . . . . . . 23
27. Duheit's panorama of
    Old Southend, *c.*1825 . . . . . . . . . . . . . . 24
28. The *Hope Hotel* . . . . . . . . . . . . . . . . . . . 24
29. The *Royal Hotel* & Royal Terrace, *c.*1900 . . 25
30. Bow Window House, *c.*1891 . . . . . . . . . . . 27
31. Plaque commemorating
    Princess Caroline's visit . . . . . . . . . . . . . 28
32. Royal Hill nameplate . . . . . . . . . . . . . . . . 28
33. Early High Street, *c.*1875 . . . . . . . . . . . . . 29
34. Sir William Heygate, 1822 . . . . . . . . . . . . . 31
35. The wooden pier, *c.*1850 . . . . . . . . . . . . . 31

36. Horse-drawn pier train, *c.*1890 . . . . . . . . . 32
37. Tithe map of Southend, 1841 . . . . . . . . . . . 33
38. St John the Baptist church, *c.*1900 . . . . . . 33
39. Tithe map of Prittlewell, 1841 . . . . . . . . . . 34
40. Southend L.T.S. (Central) station, *c.*1881-2 . 35
41. Plan of Cliff Town, *c.*1850 . . . . . . . . . . . . 36
42. Nelson Terrace . . . . . . . . . . . . . . . . . . . . 37
43. Clifftown Congregational
    Church, *c.*1890s . . . . . . . . . . . . . . . . . . 38
44. Grave of James Heygate . . . . . . . . . . . . . . 39
45. Public Hall being completed, *c.*1872 . . . . . . 39
46. Queens Road/Princes
    Street junction, 1924 . . . . . . . . . . . . . . 40
47. Southend Gas Company
    employees, *c.*1905 . . . . . . . . . . . . . . . . 41
48. Southend Waterworks, 1923 . . . . . . . . . . . 42
49. 1st Edition Ordnance Survey map, 1873 . . . 43
50. National School and
    Methodist Church, 1908 . . . . . . . . . . . . 44
51. Fire Brigade, 1878 . . . . . . . . . . . . . . . . . 44
52. Southend Victoria Hospital . . . . . . . . . . . . 47
53. Prittlewell Parish Burial Ground . . . . . . . . 47
54. Officials at the opening of the
    G.E.R. line, 1889 . . . . . . . . . . . . . . . . . 48
55. New iron pier and tollhouse, *c.*1893 . . . . . . 49
56. Electric trains on pier . . . . . . . . . . . . . . . 50
57. Thomas Dowsett, 1892 . . . . . . . . . . . . . . 51
58. Marine Parade, 1911 . . . . . . . . . . . . . . . . 52
59. Western Esplanade, 1904 . . . . . . . . . . . . . 53
60. Eastern Esplanade, 1908 . . . . . . . . . . . . . 54
61. The Cliff Lift . . . . . . . . . . . . . . . . . . . . . 54
62. Hamlet Court Road, 1907 . . . . . . . . . . . . 55
63. Westborough Road/West Road junction . . 55
64. Ramuz Drive, 1908 . . . . . . . . . . . . . . . . . 56
65. London Road/Crowstone Road junction . . 56
66. Chalkwell Esplanade, 1903 . . . . . . . . . . . . 57
67. Population figures, 1801-1901 . . . . . . . . . . 57
68. Southchurch church, *c.*1908 . . . . . . . . . . . 58
69. The *White Horse*, Southchurch, 1914 . . . . 59
70. Southchurch Hall . . . . . . . . . . . . . . . . . . 59
71. Thorpe Hall, *c.*1861 . . . . . . . . . . . . . . . . 60
72. 2nd Edition Ordnance Survey map, 1898 . . 61

73. Southchurch Boulevard, 1913 . . . . . . . . . . 62
74. Thorpe Hall Avenue bridge, 1914 . . . . . . . 63
75. Pier Hill Buildings, c.1897 . . . . . . . . . . . . 64
76. Pierhead extension promenade
      under construction, 1908 . . . . . . . . . . . . 64
77. *Palace Theatre* and *Plough*, 1922 . . . . . . . . 65
78. Southend United plaque . . . . . . . . . . . . . . 65
79. Pier Hill Fairground, c.1893 . . . . . . . . . . . 66
80. Kursaal, showing Warwick Tower, c.1905 . . 66
81. Tylers Avenue Fire Station, 1906 . . . . . . . . 67
82. Sutton Road, 1914 . . . . . . . . . . . . . . . . . 68
83. Sutton Road Cemetery, 1895 . . . . . . . . . . 68
84. Technical School, c.1910 . . . . . . . . . . . . . 69
85. Bournemouth Park School, 1908 . . . . . . . . 70
86. Public Library, 1912 . . . . . . . . . . . . . . . . 71
87. St Erkenwald's, 1995 . . . . . . . . . . . . . . . . 71
88. Garon's Shop in the High Street, 1912 . . . . 72
89. Board announcing the construction
      of the *Hotel Metropole*, c.1892 . . . . . . . . . 73
90. Thorpe Esplanade, 1911 . . . . . . . . . . . . . . 74
91. Leigh Road at Chalkwell Park, 1912 . . . . . 75
92. Leigh Church, c.1893 . . . . . . . . . . . . . . . . 76
93. Essex Regiment, 1915 . . . . . . . . . . . . . . . 78
94. Zeppelin damage, 1915 . . . . . . . . . . . . . . 79
95. Mayor Joseph Francis and Chief
      Constable, H.M.Kerslake, 1914 . . . . . . . 80
96. Eastwood Road, 1913 . . . . . . . . . . . . . . . 81
97. Southbourne Grove, 1914 . . . . . . . . . . . . . 81
98. Prince Avenue, looking west near
      Dulverton Avenue, 1921 . . . . . . . . . . . . 82
99. Priory Crescent, 1923 . . . . . . . . . . . . . . . 83
100. Eastern Avenue, 1926 . . . . . . . . . . . . . . . 83
101. Cuckoo Corner, 1923 . . . . . . . . . . . . . . . 84
102. Prittlewell Chase, 1922 . . . . . . . . . . . . . . 84
103. Eastwood Lane, 1915 . . . . . . . . . . . . . . . 85
104. Victoria Avenue, 1923 . . . . . . . . . . . . . . . 86
105. R.A. Jones . . . . . . . . . . . . . . . . . . . . . . 87
106. The opening of Prittlewell Priory by
      the Duke of York, 1920 . . . . . . . . . . . . 88
107. Sutton Road, 1921 . . . . . . . . . . . . . . . . . 88
108. Southchurch Hall renovations, 1929 . . . . . . 89
109. First tram to go round
      Warrior Square, 1921 . . . . . . . . . . . . . . 90
110. Trolleybus in Quebec Avenue, 1930 . . . . . . 91
111. Chalkwell Station bridge before the station
      was built, 1911 . . . . . . . . . . . . . . . . . . 92
112. Westcliff swimming baths, 1914 . . . . . . . . . 93
113. Marine Parade, 1924 . . . . . . . . . . . . . . . . 94
114. The opening of the pier extension, 1929 . . 95
115. Western sunken gardens and pier, 1923 . . . 95
116. *Strand* cinema, 1921 . . . . . . . . . . . . . . . . 96
117. High Street, looking south, 1924 . . . . . . . . 96
118. Southend General Hospital, c.1932 . . . . . . . 97

119. Eastwood church . . . . . . . . . . . . . . . . . . . 98
120. Church Road, South Shoebury, c.1930 . . . 100
121. North Shoebury church . . . . . . . . . . . . . . 101
122. Fox Hall Farmhouse . . . . . . . . . . . . . . . . 101
123. 3rd Edition Ordnance Survey map, 1923 . 102
124. Earls Hall Estate from the air, 1931 . . . . . 103
125. Southend Airport, c.1953 . . . . . . . . . . . . 104
126. Auxiliary Fire Service, c.1940 . . . . . . . . . . 105
127. Second World War blocks . . . . . . . . . . . . 106
128. Campbell Road bomb damage, 1941 . . . . 107
129. Bomb damage in Southend, 1942 . . . . . . . 108
130. Wartime rescue vehicle, 1943 . . . . . . . . . 110
131. The new pier trains, 1949 . . . . . . . . . . . . 111
132. Proclamation of the Accession of
      Queen Elizabeth II, 1952 . . . . . . . . . . 112
133. The *Cliffs Pavilion* . . . . . . . . . . . . . . . . . 113
134. Flooding on the seafront, 1953 . . . . . . . . 114
135. Southchurch Road, c.1951 . . . . . . . . . . . . 116
136. The 'Road to the West' bridge at Leigh . 118
137. St Christopher's Special School, 1959 . . . . 119
138. The Queen Mother opening the new
      Council Chamber, 1967 . . . . . . . . . . . . 120
139. The new Public Library . . . . . . . . . . . . . . 121
140. The Queen Mother outside the new
      Civic Centre, 1967 . . . . . . . . . . . . . . . 121
141. Map showing proposed route of the
      Ring Road, 1960 . . . . . . . . . . . . . . . . . 123
142. Ring Road under construction, 1966 . . . . 124
143. Park Street railway bridge . . . . . . . . . . . . 124
144. Porters Grange underpass nearing
      completion, 1977 . . . . . . . . . . . . . . . . . 125
145. High Street, c.1966 . . . . . . . . . . . . . . . . . 126
146. Newly pedestrianised High Street, c.1968 . 126
147. Technical College and Hammerson
      development, c.1970 . . . . . . . . . . . . . . . 127
148. Technical College demolition, 1971 . . . . . 128
149. Southend Pier fire, 1976 . . . . . . . . . . . . . 130
150. New (1986) pier trains . . . . . . . . . . . . . . 131
151. The Royals shopping centre under
      construction, 1987 . . . . . . . . . . . . . . . . 132
152. Site for Sainsbury's supermarket, 1987 . . . . 132
153. Eastwood housing brochure, c.1980 . . . . . 133
154. North Shoebury development . . . . . . . . . . 134
155. The new Tesco's supermarket, 1995 . . . . . 135
156. New (1995) hospital wing . . . . . . . . . . . . 135
157. Old Keddie's site, 1997 . . . . . . . . . . . . . 136
158. Southend Airshow, 2001 . . . . . . . . . . . . . 137
159. Borough Centenary celebrations, 1992 . . . 137
160. Southend seafront from the air, 1995 . . . . 138
161. Garon Leisure Park construction, c.1993 . . 138
162. Gas works site, 2001 . . . . . . . . . . . . . . . . 140
163. New lifeboat station and sundeck, 2001 . . 140
164. The new town square, 2001 . . . . . . . . . . . 141

# Acknowledgements

The illustrations in this book are reproduced by courtesy of the following: Edward Clack, 4, 161; Essex Police Museum/Essex Record Office, 95, 114, 128-9, 132, 134-5, 137; Essex Record Office, 18, 20, 23, 30, 33-7, 39, 41-2, 47, 49, 51-2, 54, 56-7, 72, 75, 79-81, 92-3, 105, 120, 123, 131, 147-8; John Manning/Essex Record Office, 126; Jessie Payne Collection/Janet Purdy/Southend-on-Sea Borough Libraries, 24; Phillimore & Co. Ltd., 16, 26; PhotoVisual/Southend Borough Council, 155, 160; Southend Borough Council, 5, 83, 125, 138, 140-2, 144-6, 151; Southend Borough Council/Essex Record Office, 15, 46, 48, 50, 58-60, 62-6, 69, 73-4, 76-7, 82, 84-5, 88, 90-1, 96-104, 107-13, 115-7, 130; Southend Museums Service, 1-2, 6-8, 11; Southend Museums Service/Essex Record Office, 27; Southend-on-Sea Borough Libraries, 40, 45, 86, 89, 124; Thorpe Hall Golf Club, 71. All other pictures are from the author's collection. All efforts have been made to trace the copyright holders for 105, 126, 131, 141, 147, 148, 153. If any of these illustrations are still within copyright I apologise to all concerned.

Apart from the purely numerical acknowledgements, I would particularly like to thank Jennifer Butler, Sarah Ball & colleagues at the Essex Record Office, Ken Crowe & colleagues at Southend Central Museum, Susan Gough & colleagues at Southend Library and Martin Scott & colleagues at Southend Borough Council for the immense amount of time and effort they put in to help me with my research. This book would have been poorer without their involvement.

Equally importantly, I would like to thank my wife, Alison, for her help in typing the manuscript – it would not have been finished on time without her.

I would also like to thank Noel Osborne and colleagues at Phillimore for considering me for the book in the first place and for being so understanding at difficult points during its research and writing.

Finally, I would like to thank the following for their help at specific points during the project: Edward Clack; John Durrant/Lillian Holmes; Essex Police Museum/Catherine Marshall; Fred Nash; Janet Purdy; the Port of London Authority; Sister Mary & the Sisters of Nazareth; Southend United Football Club; Thorpe Hall Golf Club; staff at Chelmsford library; the ministers, church officials and congregations at various local churches; and the numerous Southend people who offered me information during my researches.

*One*

# Early History

It is a curious paradox of Southend's history that much of its past has been revealed by its development – as the town and borough expanded, so more and more land was opened up for building. The brickfields which accompanied this expansion, particularly those in Shoebury, Thorpe Bay and Southchurch, have revealed a wealth of prehistoric finds and the Shoebury fields in particular (which covered a large part of mainly North Shoebury) have revealed a great deal about Southend's past, particularly from the Stone, Bronze and Iron Ages.

## Stone Age

The earliest settlers in the area covered by the modern borough of Southend were evidently attracted to this south-east corner of the county by both the ease of access from the river (Thames) and, when cultivation began, by the fertility of the soil. Finds from all ages dating back to the late Stone Age have been made across the borough and there is evidence of intensive farming from this period onwards.

Numerous finds of implements such as axes have been made throughout the area and there is evidence of trading links between south-east Essex and other parts of Britain and the Continent.

## Bronze Age

Significant Bronze-Age finds in the borough include a 'Beaker' burial discovered at Thorpe Hall brickfield in the 1920s (dating from 2000-1700BC and so named from the distinctive 'beaker'-style

**1** Palaeolithic hand axes – just some of the Stone-Age finds made in the area covered by the modern Southend Borough.

**2**   Part of a 'Bronze-Age hoard' of items uncovered at Leigh-on-Sea.

pottery in common use in this period) and a whole array of 'hoards' from as far apart as Shoebury and Leigh. These hoards, consisting primarily of scrap tools (mainly axes) and weapons (spears, knives, etc.), exist in a surprisingly high concentration in the Southend area and, although the purpose of their burial is unclear, they are very important to the study of this period.

Trade with the Continent, including areas of Central Europe, was evidently taking place in this era, too, and several complete Bronze-Age pots have been found. Much of Southchurch during this period was covered by a lagoon (stretching from approximately the old gasworks site on the seafront to Bournes Green) and there is evidence – a mound of discarded shells (from a shellfish diet) – of inhabitation on the edges of the lagoon at this time.

Apart from 'finds', other evidence of Late Bronze-Age/Early Iron-Age activity in the area is provided by so-called 'camps' – enclosures of ditches and ramparts which may have had domestic or military use. Arguably the most important is at Fossetts Farm in the north of the

borough (behind Waitrose), which is a Scheduled Ancient Monument. Recorded in some documents as 'Prittlewell Camp', this is a rather inconspicuous area of trees and undulations, but beneath the undergrowth one can find traces of the original enclosure.

The camp appears to have the form of a circular hill-fort (there are good views from here north and east towards the River Roach), measuring as much as 800 feet in diameter. Much of the original enclosure has been ploughed, but the best-preserved area, the south-western corner, still retains a clearly defined ditch and ramparts. From the bottom of the ditch to the top of the rampart is at least six feet in some places. In the south-eastern corner there is a raised mound, about six feet high, which appears to date from a later period, possibly as late as medieval, as pottery from that period was found in it during a cursory examination in the 1920s when some Late Bronze-Age pottery was found elsewhere on the site. The use of part of the camp as a rubbish tip in the 1920s has not helped with clear dating and identification – detailed excavation is required.

**3** Earthworks at Fossetts Farm – a Late Bronze-Age or Early Iron-Age hill-fort.

At the time of writing, plans are being considered for a new Southend United football stadium in the area and the club's proposals include a full excavation of the camp and the erection of information boards.

Aerial photography has revealed another suspected Late Bronze-Age camp in the fields about a mile to the east of Fossetts Farm (to the north of the section of Eastern Avenue now renamed Royal Artillery Way), but this area has yet to be excavated.

**4** An aerial view of a suspected Late Bronze-Age camp off Eastern Avenue (Royal Artillery Way), yet to be properly investigated.

**5** Excavations in the late 1990s at the Iron-Age camp at Shoebury Garrison.

## Iron Age

One of the most significant archaeological discoveries in Southend in recent years has been that of an Iron-Age camp at Shoebury Garrison. Traditionally, the site had been thought to be a 'Danish Camp', built by forces retreating from the Battle of Benfleet in *c*.AD893, but extensive excavations in the late 1990s, when the Garrison was being put up for sale, have revealed beyond doubt that the camp is Iron-Age. Finds from other periods (including the Stone and Bronze Ages) have also been made there, but nothing of Danish origin, so it could be that the Danes stopped somewhere else on this coast (they are recorded in the *Anglo-Saxon Chronicle* as being here) or perhaps they reused the Iron-Age fort but did not stay long enough to leave any trace?

The Shoebury camp is also a Scheduled Ancient Monument, but only two sections of its perimeter bank remain; parts of it were destroyed in the early 1850s when the Garrison firing range was first set up in this vicinity, and part has been lost to coastal erosion. The overall length (north-south) would be around 1,500 feet; the width is difficult to determine because of the loss of land to the sea. The two surviving stretches of rampart are as much as six feet high in places, and the now-filled-in ditch around them was found in the 19th century to be around nine feet deep. Perhaps most significantly, evidence of Iron-Age roundhouses and trades such as spinning and weaving was found during the late 1990s, and the main period of occupation, dated from these activities and pottery finds, appears to have been *c*.400-200BC. There is also evidence of extensive trading with southern central England and beyond.

Evidence of Iron-Age occupation elsewhere in the borough has been found at North Shoebury, Bournes Green, Temple Farm and Hastings Road. These sites have all revealed Iron-Age finds, mostly of pottery. The Temple Farm site has also revealed evidence of an Iron-Age house and gold staters ('coins' without monetary value, but indicating wealth). In the 1920s a collection of Iron-Age pots and cremation burials was found near Prittle Brook on the Roots Hall Estate.

## Romans

The 1990s excavations at the Garrison revealed several Roman finds, including a 'substantial Romanised structure' incorporating wattle-and-daub walls and a tiled roof. Roman coins and pottery in this vicinity were previously found in the 1930s.

Roman pottery and coins have been found across the borough, from Leigh to Shoebury, and a substantial burial group was found east of Priory Park, close to the railway line, when in 1923 Priory Crescent was being built. Roman pottery kilns were found in the Shoebury brickfields in 1892-5 and a stone Roman head has also been found at Shoebury. Reused Roman bricks exist in the wall of Prittlewell church.

There has been speculation that a Roman fort (part of a chain of 'Forts of the Saxon Shore', designed to repel Saxon invaders) once existed off

6   A Roman flagon, found in the Southend area.

Shoeburyness or nearby Foulness Island but, if it ever existed, it has been lost to the sea. Extensive Roman finds have also been made just outside the borough, notably at Wakering and Canvey.

The Romans used the River Thames for transport and may well have cultivated oysters off Southend. There is evidence that they carried out salt manufacture from seawater in the Garrison area.

## Saxons

When the Roman cemetery was found in 1923 during the construction of Priory Crescent, a Saxon cemetery was located in the same vicinity. (This juxtaposition appears to be a coincidence.) The Saxon cemetery, which has been dated to the sixth and seventh centuries, revealed pottery, weapons and brooches, many of which are on display at the Central Museum.

7   A 1923 photograph of workmen excavating the newly discovered Saxon cemetery at Prittlewell.

**8** Saxon pendants found at Prittlewell's Saxon cemetery.

Other notable Saxon finds have been made in North Shoebury and in the old Thorpe Hall brickfields, where some silver coins were located. Odd finds have been made across the borough, including at West Street in Leigh in the 1890s where more Saxon coins were found.

Perhaps the most famous and most visible evidence of Saxon occupation in Southend is the arch in the north wall of Prittlewell church. Many local place-names also provide evidence of Saxon occupation.

**9** The Saxon arch in the north wall of Prittlewell church.

# Two

# Prittlewell

By Saxon times all six historic communities that form modern-day Southend borough were in existence. Prittlewell, Southchurch, Leigh, Eastwood, North Shoebury and South Shoebury were all established, as was Milton, once a parish in its own right, later a part of Prittlewell.

The parish system originated with the Saxons and the whole of the village settlement pattern in south-east Essex was probably complete by the late seventh century. Many local placenames still provide evidence of their Saxon origins.

Prittlewell, the mother parish of Southend, was particularly well established. The Saxon cemetery and the Saxon arch in the north wall of the parish church provide evidence that there was a community here before the Norman Conquest, whilst the parish's name is Saxon for a babbling spring or brook – the spring arising in one of the ponds in what is now Priory Park.

The cemetery evidence shows that the village's origins date from at least the seventh century and there have been claims that a Saxon church on the site of the present building was constructed at the instigation of St Cedd, responsible for building similar seventh-century churches at Bradwell and Tilbury. The Saxon arch in the north wall of the present church could well be a survival from this period.

**Prittlewell Church – St Mary the Virgin**

Prittlewell church saw several changes after its Saxon origins, as the village around it grew. The Royal Commission on Historic Monuments in 1923 described it as being 'of considerable architectural

**10** Prittlewell church, showing the distinctive 15th-century pinnacled tower.

**11**  A model of how Prittlewell Priory might have looked, based on archaeological evidence. The western (top) and southern (left) sides of the courtyard are the only remaining complete sections.

interest from its variety of styles'. Philip Benton, the celebrated author of a history of Rochford Hundred (the administrative district in which Prittlewell lay), thought it the 'fairest and largest in the Hundred'.

In the late 11th or early 12th century a new Norman church (incorporating the Saxon arch and presumably parts of the surrounding wall) was erected on the site and the north wall of the nave and the chancel survive from this period. Later in the 12th century a new partial south aisle was added, with arcades being pierced through the old south wall. This aisle was expanded massively in the late 15th or early 16th century and a new south-east chapel, known as the Jesus Chapel, after the Jesus Guild which operated there, was also introduced. The difference in building periods between the old and new south aisles can clearly be seen in the columns in the nave.

The 15th century also saw the addition of the distinctive pinnacled tower, which was probably completed *c*.1470, before the south aisle was extended. The tower soon became important as a recognisable landmark for sailors. A south porch was also added to the newly-built south aisle. Much of the stone used for the building was brought across the river from Kent, and some came from Lincolnshire.

The church was subject to extensive restoration in 1870-1, but much survives from earlier periods. Blocked Norman windows can be seen above the arcading on the south side of the nave and traces of other Norman windows can be found in the north wall.

The list of vicars shows the earliest incumbent in 1323, though there is evidence of an appointment from late in the previous century. Other items of interest inside the church include a 13th-century coffin lid, some 14th-century wooden panels from

**12**   Prittlewell Priory, showing the surviving refectory (left) and Prior's Chamber, plus some of the foundations of the other buildings. (Compare this with picture 11.)

an old money chest, the 16th-century octagonal font and the remains of the rood stairs. The three oldest of the 10 bells date from 1603, though they have all been recast. The best of the wall monuments is that in the nave to Mary Davies, which dates from 1623.

Perhaps the church's finest treasure is the stained glass in the Jesus Chapel, dating from the 16th century and brought to Prittlewell from the church of St Ouen at Rouen in France. It was sold during the French Revolution and was ultimately acquired by the Neave family, on whose behalf it was installed in the 1880s to commemorate Sir Arundell Neave. It is possible that some of the glass is the work of the celebrated German artist, Albrecht Durer.

## Prittlewell Priory

In the early 12th century, probably *c*.1110, Prittlewell's lord of the manor, Robert de Essex (son of Sweyn, who held the manor of Prittlewell at the time of Domesday Book), gave a grant of land at Prittlewell to the Cluniac Priory at Lewes for the establishment of a new priory in south-east Essex. The Priory was built on open land on the other side of Prittle Brook below Prittlewell village.

Modern excavations have shown that the construction of the priory buildings probably took place piecemeal, beginning with wooden structures and progressing to stone as funds allowed. The first building was probably a small oratory with apsidal (rounded) ends. Eventually the completed priory included a church and cloisters, a chapter-house, chapels, refectory and cellars, numerous outbuildings for ancillary activities and some fishponds. The whole complex may have been enclosed by a wall to keep the monks secluded from the villagers.

Despite its size there were at most only 18 monks at the priory at one time. The position of

Prior was often honorary, as the Prior was not always resident. In addition to their daily religious devotions the monks mostly wrote and copied books, and employed servants and labourers for manual work.

As a Cluniac priory and therefore ultimately subservient, via the chief English priory at Lewes, to the mother priory at Cluny in France, Prittlewell was regarded as an 'alien' house and frequently became a political pawn when England was at war with France. This meant that it was often taxed during wartime and had to contribute financially to the war chest, as priors also had to buy protection for their priory at times of war. The financial status of the priory consequently fluctuated over the years and the revenues of various local parishes, including Eastwood and North Shoebury, were appropriated. Tithes, parochial rights and advowsons of many other Essex places, including Milton, were also taken over.

In 1374 it was declared that Prittlewell was no longer an alien house, and would not be seized or taxed during foreign wars (though the prior had to assist with gathering soldiers together for such campaigns).

The priory survived until 1536 when it was dissolved by Henry VIII and its funds and valuables were taken by the Crown. Only seven monks were living there at the time. An inventory of the buildings and their contents was taken but shortly after this most of the buildings, including the believed 200ft-long priory church, were pulled down, leaving only the refectory, cellars and Prior's Chamber (above the cellars) standing. In subsequent centuries residential accommodation was added to the west and south-west fronts as the surviving priory buildings were converted for domestic use. The refectory contains the oldest surviving construction work – the north wall dates from the late 12th or early 13th century and features an excellent late Norman doorway with 'dog-tooth' (zig-zag) decoration.

Twentieth-century excavations revealed the foundations of some of the lost priory buildings and these are laid out in stone in the grounds of what is now Priory Park. The old monastic fish-ponds also survive and ironically are popular with anglers! The Priory itself is a museum.

## The Jesus Guild
The grant that established Prittlewell Priory included church and rectorial tithes, plus the emoluments of priests serving Prittlewell, Eastwood and Sutton churches. This impoverished Prittlewell church, particularly after the Dissolution, when the Priory was in private ownership.

To counteract some of this poverty, a so-called 'Jesus Guild' was established in the village. This was a religious guild formed by Royal Charter in the late 1470s which had its own priest-cum-school-master and did much to improve the lot of Prittlewell's villagers. The Guild partly financed the 15th-century enlargement of the parish church (possibly with some assistance from the Priory), including the building of the south aisle. The Jesus Chapel, at the eastern end of that aisle, was named after the Guild.

There was once a building at the western end of the south aisle (the blocked doorway to it remains) and it is thought that this was either the schoolroom or the lodging of the Jesus Guild's priest. Alternatively, the priest's house could have been in a separate building called Church Lodge which stood to the south of the church, next to the entrance from East Street. That building was demolished in the 1930s. A 'Jesus House' or 'Jesus Hall' also once existed in East Street, on the other side of the road. It is possible that the room over the church porch could also have been used for teaching.

Like the priory, the Jesus Guild survived until the Dissolution, when the village which it served was left to fend for itself.

## Prittlewell Village and Parish
Prittlewell village grew up at the top of 'Prittlewell Hill', where the church stands, around East, West and North Streets (the latter now part of a renamed Victoria Avenue) at the road junction now known from the pub there as the *Blue Boar*. (There was no road to the south at this time – the stretch from Prittlewell to Southend of what was to become Victoria Avenue was not built until the late 19th century.) Timber-framed buildings were clustered around the church, many actually backing onto the churchyard, but most of these were cleared between *c.*1912 and the 1930s.

**13** East Street, Prittlewell, *c.*1908, showing the buildings which once stood in front of Prittlewell church. Most of these were demolished *c.*1912-1930s, though the one at the right with the awning survives.

**14** North Street (now Victoria Avenue), Prittlewell, *c.*1913. The buildings on the right hide the church. Some of the buildings on the left still survive despite later road widening to accommodate four lanes of traffic.

**15**   The bridge over the brook at the bottom of Prittlewell Hill, pictured in 1908 when the village water pump was still in use. The road on the right next to the pump (which still survives) is now Priory Crescent and the gap between the pump and the long-gone cottage is now the entrance to Priory Park.

Water was provided from the brook at the foot of the hill (originally crossed by a ford, later a bridge) and an early 19th-century pump survives there, by the Priory Park gates. A more convenient pump supply was later set up at the top of the hill in the village near the church. Benton met an old Prittlewell resident who remembered a well collapsing *c.*1795 in the middle of the road outside the *Blue Boar*.

The main roads into Prittlewell led from London (via what is now West Road and West Street) and Rochford (via Sutton Road and East Street or Rochford Road and North Street). There was also a route to Southchurch, via East Street and Sutton Road to Southchurch Road.

There were two routes from the village to the seashore, a mile or so to the south. The first took the traveller to Southchurch Road as above, then south down what became 'Southend Lane' (roughly the route of Southchurch Avenue now, but with a bit still surviving as Old Southend Road) to 'Stratende' ('the end of the street', approximately where the Kursaal is). The other route was to the shore at Milton, going via West Street, North Road (named 'North' from the Milton perspective) and Milton Road to the sea.

Prittlewell parish was extensive and stretched from approximately a line between where are now Westcliff High School and Chalkwell Park Drive/ Grand Drive in the west (where it met Leigh

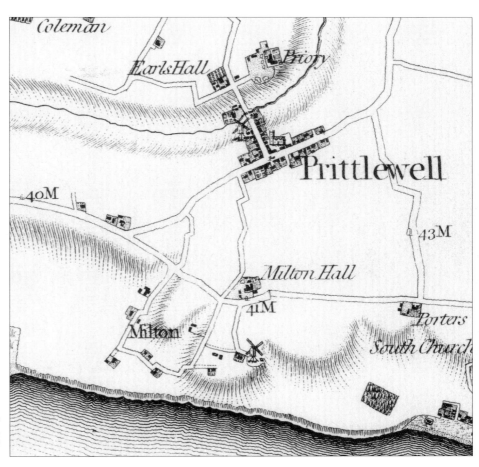

**16** Chapman and André's map of Prittlewell in 1777, showing the village centre and the major manors.

parish) to a line between Hamstel Road and Southchurch Hall in the east (Southchurch parish). It was bordered in the north-west (beyond approximately Rochford Road and Warners Bridge) by Eastwood and in the north-east (in the fields beyond what are now Temple Farm and Eastern Avenue) by Sutton and Shopland parishes. There was also a detached part of the parish on Canvey Island, which for agricultural purposes had been divided among a number of mainland parishes keen to exploit its fertile soil.

The part of the main parish south of the London Road between Grand Drive and Queensway (approximately) was the area known as Milton, originally a parish in its own right (see below).

Many modern streets in this area would not now be thought of as being in Prittlewell, a

reflection of how the parishes' boundaries have 'blurred' as Southend has grown.

The size of the parish and its church provides a good indication of the village's prominence in south-east Essex. Medieval Prittlewell, though rather remote geographically, was third only to Rochford and Rayleigh as an important south-east Essex settlement. The population of the village in the mid-16th century was around three hundred.

At least as early as the 13th century a market and a fair were both established in Prittlewell and these too helped with its growth. The weekly market closed down centuries ago – perhaps shortly before 1594 when traveller and mapmaker, John Norden, described the village as 'sometyme a market towne' – but the fair, held annually in the churchyard, lasted until at least the 1860s, after which it was closed down for being too riotous!

**17**   The entrance to Priory Park from Victoria Avenue early in the 20th century. Prior's Hall manor was based around the Priory.

### The Main Prittlewell Manors – Priors Hall and Earls Hall

Outside the village centre, the extensive lands of Prittlewell parish, held by Sweyn in 1086 at the time of Domesday Book, gradually became divided into manors.

One of these, Priors or Priors Hall, which was loosely based on the old Priory lands (effectively most of the land to the north-east of North Street (Victoria Avenue) and East Street), was granted at the Dissolution to Sir Thomas Audley, who acquired the priory buildings, manor, rectory and advowson (the right to appoint an incumbent) of Prittlewell church. Audley later sold the manor to the family of Richard, Lord Rich, a major Essex landowner who owned nearby Rochford Hall and had for many years been in the process of acquiring extensive estates throughout south-east Essex.

At his death, Rich's estate passed through his family to successive Earls of Warwick until the line died out in 1678. In that year the estates were partitioned and the Priors manor passed to Daniel, Earl of Nottingham, who sold it to Daniel Scratton, a wealthy businessman and a native of Suffolk, then living in Billericay. This began the Scratton family's long association with Prittlewell (and subsequently Southend) which would last into the 20th century. The family did a lot to shape both Prittlewell's and Southend's futures. The first proper school in Prittlewell (see below) was set up by another Daniel Scratton in the 1720s. Scratton Road is named after the family and there are monuments to various family members in Prittlewell church. In 1869 Daniel Robert Scratton sold most of the family's estates and retired to Devon.

Another Prittlewell manor was Earls-fee or Polste(a)d Wic(k), later known as Earls Hall. The manor house for this stood across the road (now Victoria Avenue) opposite the present Priory

**18**  Earls Hall, *c*.1900. This stood approximately opposite the Victoria Avenue entrance to Priory Park shown in the previous picture and was demolished in the 1960s. It is remembered in the name of a local school and surrounding streets.

entrance gates for cars and the name survives in Earls Hall Avenue and School. The manor's lands were mostly to the south and west of the priory and included Prittlewell village itself.

The 'Earls' part of the name comes from the manor's one-time owners, the de Vere family, Earls of Oxford. Part of this manor was also once in the ownership of the locally prominent de Southchurch family. The Polstead part of the manor's name may come from previous owners, though various land areas bearing the name have also been cited.

The manor of Earls Hall passed through the de Vere family until, like Priors Hall, it eventually came into the ownership of Richard, Lord Rich and then to Daniel, Earl of Nottingham. It was then sold through several owners into the hands of the Neave family. As mentioned above, Sir Arundell Neave is commemorated in stained glass in Prittlewell church.

**Milton**

Perhaps the most interesting of the major manors in Prittlewell parish was that of Milton Hall, whose manor house stood at the junction of London Road and North Road, to the south-west of Prittlewell village. The original building has long since disappeared and the site is now occupied by the extensive Nazareth House complex, run by the Catholic Sisters of Nazareth as a care and residential home for the elderly.

Milton, once a parish in its own right, held onto its independence for a long time and grew into quite a sizeable port and shipbuilding centre, with its own parish officers. Admiralty courts were also once held there. It was finally undone by coastal erosion, losing its church, port and large areas of land to the sea. According to Philip Benton, writing in the late 19th century, the now-demolished Hamlet Farm lost as much as 12 acres of its land to the sea over the years due to 'great encroachments'

**19** Nazareth House in London Road, hidden behind a high wall and occupying the site of the former Milton Hall.

of the waters. A footpath to Leigh which ran across the farm's land had to be moved back 21 rods (about 350 feet) in 60 years. A 21ft-high cliff was substantially reduced, as each year 7-8,000 tons of earth were washed away! Benton advocated the construction of a stone embankment at the foot of the cliff, lamenting that 'prudence should have dictated this measure long ago'.

Milton is acknowledged as a separate settlement in Domesday Book and was under the ownership of the monks of Holy Trinity, Canterbury, until 1539 when their Christchurch Priory was dissolved. It was later given by the Crown to Richard, Lord Rich and, like Priors Hall, it passed through the Warwick line until being purchased from the Earl of Nottingham by Daniel Scratton. It gets its name from the fact that it was the 'middle town' (corrupted to 'Milton') on this stretch of coast, lying between Southchurch and Leigh.

During its time as a port it seems to have been something of a favourite embarkation point for noblemen and priests fleeing court intrigue or religious persecution.

The minute books of the Prittlewell parish vestry (a forerunner of parish councils) record occasional differences of opinion between Prittlewell and Milton inhabitants. One of the most notable was a discussion in 1678 about whether or not Milton residents should pay towards the repair of the bridge (probably then only a footbridge) at the bottom of Prittlewell Hill. As late as 1813 discussions were still going on about whether Prittlewell and Milton were one parish. Poor Laws were administered jointly between the two in the 1830s, but highway maintenance appears to have been kept separate until the Southend Local Board was formed in 1866.

Milton once had a windmill, standing at the junction of Avenue Road and Park Road, just west of the latter and north of the later railway line, but this was demolished in the late 19th century. Avenue Road provided a direct route to the mill from Milton Hall. It appears quite clearly on Chapman and André's 1777 map.

Though now lost amid dormitory housing, the ancient community of Milton retains its identity as an electoral ward of the modern Southend borough. The road names, 'Milton Road' and 'Hamlet Court Road' also recall it (Milton was referred to in Prittlewell parish vestry minutes as 'the hamlet' to distinguish it from Prittlewell, 'the town'). (A residence, Hamlet Court, was erected in the road

**20**  Chalkwell Hall, *c*.1875, before its acquisition for a public park.

after Milton port's demise.) Chapman and André's map shows two routes to Prittlewell from Milton – one along Milton Road and North Road into West Street and the other via Hamlet Court Road and West Road.

## Chalkwell Hall

In the far west of Prittlewell parish, to modern eyes more in Westcliff or Leigh, was the manor of Chalkwell Hall. The last Hall building, still standing in what is now Chalkwell Park, is Georgian (1830) and is at least the third to go by that name, its predecessors standing further to the west in the vicinity of Leigh Road and nearer the railway. The name is believed to come from a well on the estate which was once lined with chalk – it may be on the site of the present pond to the west of the Hall – or from the liberal application of chalk to the fields for agricultural purposes. The manor remained largely remote and agricultural until *c*.1900 when a growing Southend was extending westwards.

Chalkwell Hall manor, once a sub-manor to Milton, was owned for a long period throughout the 18th and early 19th centuries by the Tyrrell family, some of whose ancestors had risen to high ranks in the nobility. The family owned much other

land and property in south Essex and Suffolk. In 1830 the manor was acquired by George Mason, who built the present Chalkwell Hall.

Much of the old Chalkwell Hall estate was developed for housing *c*.1900, at which time the Hall was retained and the grounds surrounding it were converted into gardens as Chalkwell Park.

In the river to the south of the Chalkwell Hall estate is the Crowstone, first erected in the 13th century to mark the eastern boundary of jurisdiction

**21**  The Crowstone, off Chalkwell beach. The stone formerly marked the limit of jurisdiction over the River Thames and is at least the third such stone to stand on the site.

**22** Porters (or Porters Grange) — formerly a manor of Prittlewell parish and now the civic house of Southend's mayor. The plaque on the gatepost commemorates the visits there of Benjamin Disraeli in 1833 and 1834.

of the City of London over the River Thames. There used to be a regular ceremony there, with the Lord Mayor of London in attendance, but this died out in 1856. In 1857 the Thames Conservancy Act reallocated the river's jurisdiction jointly to the City and the Crown. Today the river is looked after by the Port of London Authority and the Crowstone no longer marks any jurisdictional limits.

There have been at least three stones on the site. The present one was placed there in the 1830s. Its immediate predecessor, carrying the barely visible City arms and the no longer legible names of several Lord Mayors, is now in Priory Park.

### Temple Sutton

One further Prittlewell manor of note was Temple Sutton, which was shared between Prittlewell and Sutton parishes, with the house standing in the former and the bulk of the land in the latter. It was owned by the Knights Templar (an organisation founded during the Crusades in the early 12th century) and then later by their successors the Knights Hospitaller, who held it until the Dissolution.

In the 1540s the manor was obtained by Richard, Lord Rich and ultimately found its way through succession to Henry St John, Viscount Bolingbroke. In around 1715 it was sold to Sir Richard Child of Wanstead and passed through succession to the Tylney Long and Wellesley Pole families, who had connections with the Duke of Wellington and also owned nearby Rochford Hall. It was sold in the 1860s to James Tabor (then living at Earls Hall), a member of an important local farming family.

The Temple Sutton manor house no longer survives and the area is perhaps best-known today for being home to the Temple Farm Industrial Estate, built on some of its land.

Many of the above manors were later subdivided, but they were the principal Prittlewell parish ones from which all the others descended.

### Porters

Another Prittlewell estate, worthy of mention because its house has survived, is that of Porters or Porters Grange.

The estate formerly reached down to the sea and indeed the modern Queensway dual carriageway immediately to the west of the building occupies the site of a former creek which ran right up to Porters itself. A group of trees on the estate was once used as a seamark and it was so significant in that role that there was a court case about it when a one-time owner wanted to chop them down.

The house itself is now used as the Mayor's Parlour (or Civic House). It was probably built in the late 15th or early 16th century, and is believed to take its name from the le Porter family, one-time landowners who may well have had an earlier building on the site. It has many interesting ancient features, including trapdoors, locks, passages and beams. It is said to have a secret hiding place behind one of the downstairs chimneys and a blocked subterranean passage which once led to the creek. One of the downstairs rooms has linenfold panelling, incorporating five early 16th-century panels of faces, thought to be French and part of a set of perhaps as many as nine. How they got there is a mystery – suggestions include from a shipwreck or from another older local building.

The last private owner of Porters was a well-known architect, Sir Charles Nicholson, who found the building's history to be 'very puzzling' – a confusion of juxtaposed dates and materials. Perhaps the original construction work was stopped before being restarted, old designs were used, or older material from elsewhere was introduced.

The building's significance is confirmed by its presence on John Norden's 1594 map of Essex, which features comparatively few named buildings other than churches. The Porters estate was for a long time in the ownership of the Tyrrell and Browne families, the latter having connections with a Lord Mayor of London. The first-known owner of the present building was Humphrey Browne, who died in 1592.

The building descended through the ownership of several other families until 1868 when the estate was partitioned into lots and sold. Much of the land went for development, but fortunately the house was retained. Sir Charles Nicholson bought it in 1912 and it was sold to Southend Corporation in 1932 to ensure its preservation. It became the Civic House three years later.

## Village Development

The development of Prittlewell village throughout the medieval, Tudor and Stuart periods was generally gradual and uneventful. Prittlewell villagers are said to have taken part in the 1381 Peasants' Revolt, when Southchurch Hall was allegedly ransacked, but the evidence for this is sketchy.

In 1554, following the accession of the Catholic Queen Mary, the Prittlewell vicar, the Reverend John Thomas, was ejected from the living, no doubt for holding opposing religious views. He was restored to the post in 1558 when the Protestant Elizabeth was Queen.

Forty years later Norden recorded that fevers were prevalent on the Essex coast and it could be that they affected some Prittlewell people. North Street, West Street and East Street were all named as such by the time of his visit.

The Civil War of the 1640s largely passed by the village, though there were some minor effects and local disagreements as recorded in the minute book of the Prittlewell parish vestry. The Reverend Thomas Peck was vicar at the time and he was succeeded in 1663 by his son, Samuel.

The Reverend Samuel Peck's eight-year incumbency was eventful. In 1665 information about the plague, then raging in London, forced the cancellation of the local fair through fear that travellers would bring the disease to the village. In 1667 the parish set up a beacon to warn of seaborne attacks by the Dutch, with whom England was at war.

By the early 18th century the parish vestry was taking steps to look after the poor of Prittlewell parish, and as early as 1759 hired premises for a workhouse (discussions about it went back to the 1720s). Funds to provide purpose-built accommodation were authorised in 1786 and a building was erected in East Street, at the junction with Sutton Road. It was used until the late 1830s, by which time the 1834 Poor Law Union Act brought the poor of all the local parishes together under one Union Workhouse in Rochford. Prittlewell poor had to wear specially designed coarse grey clothing, with a large capital 'P' on it, to identify them. The building itself survived (converted into cottages) until c.1950. A former parish lock-up (an early gaol) stood next door.

Delays to the 1720s plans for the workhouse could have been caused by problems with the then vicar, the Reverend Edward Underhill, who

**23**  East Street, Prittlewell, *c*.1900, showing some of the medieval buildings. The alleyway on the right where the girls are standing leads to the church and the buildings beyond back on to the churchyard. The building in the centre of the photograph is Deeds Cottage (see next picture). The one next to it is the former Carlton Bakery, which is currently (2001) undergoing restoration. The *Blue Boar* pub can just be seen on the left (pointed roof).

was imprisoned, apparently over debts, probably around the time the workhouse was being discussed. Part of the church roof fell in during his incumbency.

From the earliest times Prittlewell village was served by several inns and three of these, the *Blue Boar*, the *Golden Lion* and the *Spread Eagle*, survive to this day (all date in name from at least the 18th century, though they are not necessarily in the original premises). The *Cock*, the *George*, the *King & Queen*, the *King's Head*, the *Swan* and the *Three Horseshoes* have all disappeared. The *King's Head* was of particular note since it backed onto the churchyard from North Street (Victoria Avenue) and was often used at fair times for plays and at other times for meetings of the parish vestry.

During the 18th and 19th centuries the village was served by at least two windmills – all had gone by the mid-1870s.

In 1727 Prittlewell gained its first proper school-house, although records of schoolmasters in the village date back to the days of the Jesus Guild. It was established jointly by the Reverend Thomas Case, curate of Prittlewell in the Reverend Underhill's absence (and rector of Southchurch), and Daniel Scratton, lord of the manor of Priors Hall, who donated land called Glynds and Mill Croft at the bottom of Prittlewell Hill (on the right going downhill, by the brook and bridge). Mill Croft was already occupied by a 'schoolmaster', so evidently some education was already being practised in the village. A further grant of land was made in 1739 and the school was enlarged to accommodate 16 pupils instead of the original ten.

Most of Prittlewell's older buildings were demolished *c*.1912-1930s, but some of them have fortunately survived. They look a little out of place now, next to more modern buildings and traffic-filled

**24** Deeds Cottage, which stood at the junction of West Street and North Street (Victoria Avenue), pictured in 1945. It was demolished later for road widening. The building on the right is the Carlton Bakery. (Compare with the previous picture.)

roads, but they serve as a reminder of what Prittlewell would have been like 300-400 years ago.

At the corner of West Street and Victoria Avenue stands a building that was most recently used as the Carlton Bakery (officially number 255 Victoria Avenue). This dates from the 16th and 17th centuries and is currently undergoing restoration following a fire in the late 1990s. Twenty yards to the north down Victoria Avenue (nos. 269-75) stands another 16th-century building, with crosswings and a later cartway. Both have modern (20th-century) shopfronts.

A third, originally 16th-century, building, Deeds Cottage, which stood immediately to the south of the Carlton Bakery at the corner of West Street, was demolished in the 1950s for traffic improvements.

The fireplace of another ancient building, the 15th-century Reynolds in West Street which was demolished in 1906, can be seen on display in Southend Central Museum.

## The 'South End'

By the 18th century Prittlewell had built on its Saxon origins and grown into an important south-east Essex community. It retained links with much of its historic past, through surviving village buildings, the old Norman priory and Milton's history as a port.

The 18th century, however, was to be a time of great change for the village, nowhere more so than in the south-eastern corner of the parish, hard-up against the boundary with Southchurch, where an oyster fisherman made a fortuitous discovery.

Things were stirring at the 'South End' of these Priors Hall lands in the old parish that would ultimately have an amazing effect on the development not just of Prittlewell, but also of the other surrounding parishes.

# Three

# The 'South End'

There was a route to the seashore at the 'South End' of the Priors Hall lands in Prittlewell parish (near what was to become the Kursaal) from earliest times. Corn was loaded onto boats there and Prittlewell villagers traditionally took gravel from the beach for local road repairs. The earliest surviving documentary evidence for the area dates from 1309 when it was known as 'Stratende', 'the end of the street'. The first reference to it as 'Sowthende' occurs in 1481.

The route from Prittlewell village to this area (hard up against the boundary with neighbouring Southchurch parish) took the traveller via East Street, Sutton Road, Southchurch Road and Southend Lane (later Old Southend Lane/Road). This latter road followed approximately the line of today's Southchurch Avenue, though part of Old Southend Road still exists a little to the west.

## Oysters

There was no significant interest in inhabiting or developing the 'South End', other than for isolated farms, until around 1700, when it was discovered by accident that the foreshore there provided an excellent breeding ground for oysters.

A local oyster fisherman named Outing (his name is preserved in 'Outing Close') discarded some oysters, which were too small for consumption, off the shore near the southern end of the lane. Returning a year later he noticed that the oysters had grown. Recognising the value of cultivating oysters on an on-going basis, he leased a large section of the foreshore and started commercial oyster layings.

From this insignificant start, the local oyster industry grew beyond all expectations. Before long the whole of the foreshore from Shoebury to Hadleigh was under oyster cultivation and a few

**25** Old Southend Road, part of the original route into 'South End'.

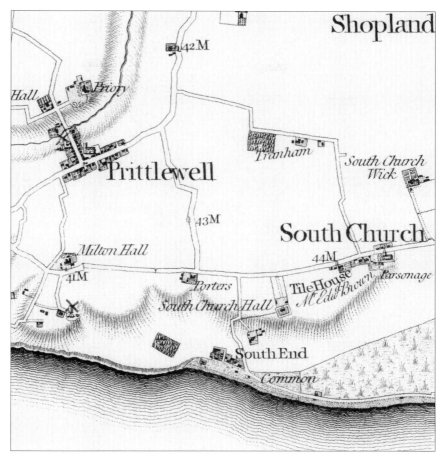

**26** Chapman and André's map of Southend, 1777, showing the new community of 'South End'.

fishermen's cottages – the first permanent dwellings in South End – were built at the end of the road from Prittlewell. This was the first step in establishing South End as a permanent community.

As time went on, new properties were built west of South End (Southend) Lane, including houses, pubs and shops. The first brick-built cottages were constructed in 1767 for the oyster fishermen by John Remnant, who farmed Thames Farm (which stood to the east of Southend Lane). These cottages were known as Pleasant Row and survived until the 1950s (Pleasant Row has been renamed Ash Walk).

The oyster industry lasted until the turn of the 20th century, when its decline was precipitated by sewage pollution from the growing Southend town.

**South End village**

The south end of Prittlewell parish was at this stage completely agricultural. Much of the land to the east of Southend Lane belonged to Facons or Fauns Farm, later Thames or Arnold's Farm (the latter named after a late 19th-century owner, Thomas Arnold). The land immediately to the west of the Lane, 'Arthur's Land' (itself named after a former owner), would be amongst the first places to be built on as the new South End community grew. Here Pleasant Row, the *Ship Hotel* and many other buildings would be built.

As the 18th century progressed, the hamlet started by Outing and his fellow oyster fishermen began to spread westwards, along what is now Marine Parade, towards the foot of what would later become Pier Hill.

**27**   Duheit's panorama of Old Southend, *c.*1825. This is probably the best early visual representation of the town, showing (towards the right) Old Southend Road and (towards the left) Pier Hill — and all the buildings in between. Several of them survive, including the *Hope Hotel* (centre) and the *Minerva* (at the corner of Old Southend Road). Even New Southend, with its *Royal Hotel* on the clifftop (far left) is shown.

Several surviving seafront pubs date from this period. The *Ship Hotel*, originally a private house, had its origins in the 1760s (though the present building – recently renamed *Image* – is a modern one). The *Hope* (still largely original) arrived *c.*1790. Beginning life as a coffee house, it was used for a time as the venue for courts of the manor of Milton Hall (in which it lay). This was swiftly followed by the *Minerva*, formerly known as 'the Great House' and owned by the barge-owning Vandervoord family who named it after one of their vessels. This, too, was once a venue for manor courts, this time for Priors Hall. The *Britannia* was also built around this time.

### New South-End

By the latter half of the 18th century sea-bathing was becoming fashionable. Scarborough, Brighton

**28**   The *Hope Hotel*, one of the oldest surviving buildings on the seafront.

and Margate were all finding success as resorts, a development which sprang from the earlier fashion for drinking water at spas and evolved into a view that drinking and bathing in seawater were equally good for one's health. As time went on Scarborough's development was checked by its remoteness from London, but Brighton and Margate, along with Weymouth (a summer resort for those originally attracted to the spa at Bath), began to grow beyond all expectations.

In 1768 a proposal was put forward to create a new sea bathing resort at South End. Nothing came of it, but the town does appear to have been receiving some good local patronage as a resort by the 1780s, helped perhaps by the presence of a crystallising salt factory, known locally as 'The Laboratory', which drew attention to the medicinal qualities of South End seawater.

By 1790 there was renewed interest in developing South End as a resort. The village had grown to around two dozen houses, with an estimated population of 125 and an established barge trade to London. The London-Rochford coach service had been extended to the village for the summer seasons, stopping at the *Ship Hotel*. It was a relatively easy place to get to from the capital – the roads were decent and there was also direct river access. Its handy location was to prove a key asset in the growth from a village into a town.

As resort proposals grew, the lord of the manor (of Milton), Daniel Scratton, sold three pieces of

land on the cliffs to the west of the town on 99-year leases for the development of a hotel and high quality houses. This new *Grand* or *Capitol Hotel* and Terrace, with coach-houses behind, was constructed in 1791-3 by the principal developers, Pratt, Watts & Lowdoun. To the east of this was another development of only slightly inferior housing – Grove Terrace (it was built on the site of a cleared grove of trees) – and there was provision for a library. A field to the west in the Shorefield area was used for brickearth extraction. The scheme included both the construction of a road down the hill to link the new development with the old fishing village and the laying out of a new north-south road through the centre of the clifftop terraces to connect South End with the London Road. This road, which would later become the High Street, included two new inns, the *Duchess of York* and the *Duke of Clarence*, both completed in 1792.

**29**    The *Royal Hotel*, *c.*1900, just over a century after its construction.

To distinguish the new clifftop resort from the old fishing village below it to the east, the term 'New South-End' came into being (sometimes hyphenated, sometimes not), with the original village becoming 'Old South-End' (ditto). The two settlements were also referred to as 'Upper' and 'Lower' South-End respectively, from their geographical positions.

The Reverend Thomas Archer, curate of Prittlewell at this time, saw much potential for the new town and penned an epic poem championing the resort and looking forward to the day when New South-End would expand as its popularity grew.

'South of the village [Prittlewell],' wrote Archer in the second (1794) version of his poem, 'but within its bound / The recent fabricks proudly rise around.'

> Here the new buildings uniformly planned,
> With southern aspect regularly stand.
> Disposed with neatness, symmetry and taste,
> In happy site and order aptly placed.

Perhaps the most famous lines from Archer's poem are those predicting the growth of the town…

> Here with prophetic view the Bard decries,
> Streets shall extend and lofty domes arise,
> Till New South-End in each spectator's eye,
> With Weymouth, Margate or Brighthelmstone [Brighton] vie.

The *Gentleman's Magazine* of the same year shared Archer's optimism, noting that New South-End was 'rising rapidly into repute', being 'remarkable for the peculiar beauty of its situation'.

Despite this optimism, however, there were a few teething problems, most of them financial. In 1792 the lease of the *Grand Hotel* and Terrace was assigned by Pratt, Watts & Lowdoun to Thomas Holland, a solicitor and builder who had already had some involvement in the scheme. A grand opening ball was held in the Assembly Room at the hotel in July 1793, but Holland's financial position was not strong. Estimates for the success of the New South-End scheme appear to have been over-optimistic and not all the houses on the terrace were taken.

John Sanderson, the Grove Terrace developer, was in a similar position. At his death in 1792 his leases were conveyed to Jeremiah Blakeman, a timber merchant, who, like Holland, had already had some involvement with the New South-End scheme. Blakeman completed Grove House – a detached residence set back from the rest and approached by a north-south avenue running parallel with the High Street – but could not afford to finish Grove Terrace itself.

By the time of Archer's poem, Holland and Blakeman were in serious financial trouble. In 1795 Holland was declared bankrupt. Building work ceased and much of his property and materials were sold off to pay creditors. Blakeman was declared bankrupt the following year.

In 1797 a mutiny at the Nore (a sandbank in the estuary to the south-east of the town where the English naval fleet frequently anchored) drew much adverse publicity, when the leading mutineers took shore leave in the town. They allegedly used the *Ship* (some sources say the *Hope*) *Hotel* as their unofficial headquarters. That year the *Grand Hotel* was forced to close due to continuing financial problems and things began to look very bleak indeed for the new resort.

This was, however, only a temporary setback. In 1799 the hotel reopened with a new licensee and the following year the remainder of Holland's estate was partitioned and sold at auction. Blakeman's estate was sold in 1802. One of the chief purchasers of the auctioned land was James Heygate, a London banker. He and his heirs were to have a significant influence on the future development of New South-End.

**Consolidation**

By 1800, after a slightly shaky start, New Southend – as the name soon became – had begun to assume the shape that would characterise it for the next few decades. The estates developed by Holland and Blakeman occupied high land either side of a new central High Street and stood out as proud advertisements for the town to those passengers on boats heading downriver to Margate.

Behind these imposing terraces, a couple of embryonic roads were forming. On the east of the High Street, behind (north of) Grove House, were market gardens and Market Road. This latter, leaving the High Street by the *Duchess of York* inn, would become York Street and later York Road.

**30** An unusual view of Marine Parade, *c.*1891, showing Bow Window House on the left. The arches below the lower end of Pier Hill can also be seen. The picture gives a good feel for the atmosphere of Old Southend in the late 19th century.

Almost opposite, on the west side of the High Street near the *Duke of Clarence* inn, was a gap where another new road – Clarence Street – would later appear.

As time went on and New Southend became ever more popular, the *Grand Hotel* was expanded into neighbouring properties. On the opposite corner a library was established by Renneson & Tarry. Grove House saw a short spell as a boarding school. Odd shops began to appear in the High Street – a butcher's and a baker's both opened near the Clarence Street junction. Houses began to spring up in both Market Road and Grove Road (the street from the Terrace to the House).

The new resort began to attract a high class of visitor and it was soon very fashionable among London gentry. Several titled individuals – lords, ladies, admirals and captains – visited the resort during the next few summer seasons and it was

fast becoming established as one of *the* sea-bathing places.

The development of New Southend also benefited the fishing village at Old Southend (as that soon became called), which doubled in size to around 50 houses by 1800. In addition to the *Ship* and *Hope Hotels*, there were also several shops and much activity connected with the London barge trade. The impressive Bow Window House was built in the 1790s at the foot of the hill leading to New Southend. It was owned at one time by Lady Charlotte Denys. It is still there, but has now been converted into the Sunspot amusement arcade – the bow windows above can still be seen.

The 1790s also saw the opening of the Caroline Baths (named after the then Princess of Wales) which stood at the far eastern end of Old Southend (approximately where the Sea Life Centre is now) and confirmed the old village's ability to attract bathers as much as the new resort's. These Baths

**31** A plaque in Royal Terrace commemorating the visit of Princess Caroline which made fledgling South End the place to go for the London aristocracy and led to the renaming of the *Grand Hotel* and Terrace.

services respectively and a whole host of attractions for the visitor. True, Southend had card games, a billiard room, bathing machines, dancing and pleasant clifftop walks, but it had little else to entice the visitor in a very competitive market. Life centred on the *Grand Hotel* and its Assembly Room, and the library over the road with its London and provincial newspapers and raffles.

A theatre was seen as a possible key attraction; a temporary one opened at the *Grand Hotel* in 1799. Plays were also put on in Old Southend, initially in temporary premises and later, in 1804, in a permanent, purpose-built structure (east of the *Minerva*, opposite the Caroline Baths) under the energetic management of Thomas Trotter.

There was much potential for the development of the new resort. River travel was less tiring and more picturesque than road transport and Margate, the key river resort with which Southend was in competition, was almost twice as far from London. The shorter journey was consequently cheaper and Southend had a sun-facing southern aspect which

constantly supplied both hot and cold bathing water – particularly useful in a tidal resort and in common use at resorts elsewhere.

Southend (as New and Old Southend together soon came to be called) was growing apace, but it was nevertheless in need of new attractions. As a new entrant to the seaside resort industry it was competing with the established resorts of Brighton and Margate which had regular coach and boat

**32** The faded nameplate of Royal Hill survives (left), though the street is now more commonly known as Pier Hill.

Margate lacked. With a growing infrastructure, including such niceties as a postal service, Southend just needed a spark to lift it into the big time.

## Royal Patronage

In 1801 five-year-old Princess Charlotte, daughter of the Prince of Wales (later George IV) and second-in-line to the throne, was sent to Southend on medical grounds and stayed at Southchurch Lawn (now Eton House School) in Southchurch, the neighbouring parish to the east of Prittlewell. She visited Southend to bathe in the waters and also attended a service at Southchurch church, taken by the former Prittlewell curate, Thomas Archer, now incumbent at Southchurch. The confidence of royal doctors in the efficacy of the waters of Southend was a clear sign to the aristocracy that here was a good place to go to for health reasons.

In 1803 or 1804 (possibly both) Charlotte's mother Caroline, the Princess of Wales, came to Southend with her retinue and stayed for three months in three houses in Grand Terrace. Other resorts had benefited from Royal patronage and New Southend was to benefit too. As a mark of her visit, the names of the hotel, terrace and library were all changed to 'Royal' and the hill connecting the Upper and Lower Towns was named Royal Hill (still today technically its correct name despite being more commonly known as Pier Hill).

In 1805, Nelson's mistress, Lady Hamilton, stayed in what was now Royal Terrace and held a ball in the honour of the Admiral.

These two high-profile events gave Southend the caché that was needed and high-class visitors began to pour into the town.

## Growth

As time went on, Southend became ever busier. Coach services from London became more frequent and a shortage of accommodation meant that people had to stay in farms and houses dotted around the district. A pattern developed: the town was packed in summer and empty in winter.

Guests such as Lady Charlotte Denys and Lady Langham visited the town, which was now at its peak period as a genteel resort for the fashionable and wealthy. The theatre was booming under the guidance of its new manager, Samuel Jerrold, and the town even received a mention in one of the classic novels of the period, *Emma*, by Jane Austen (1816). Two years earlier the landscape painter, John Constable, visited the area.

**33** The lower end of Southend High Street, pictured *c*.1875. Buildings are by now stretching up the High Street towards the London Road.

By 1824 Southend was of sufficient repute and size to warrant its own guidebook. It was described as 'a place which is rapidly rising in public estimation', with comfortable hotels and neat rows of dwelling/lodging houses in both the Upper and Lower Towns. There were a Post Office and shops in the Old Town, a theatre, bathing machines and a warm bath at the *Ship Hotel*, and a grass promenade between the buildings and the beach.

The New Town was prospering equally, houses sprang up on the High Street and the now *'Royal' Hotel* did a roaring trade. There was a broad open gravel terrace in front of the hotel and below that a network of woodland paths through a 'Shrubbery', beneath which, on the beach, were warm baths and bathing machines reserved exclusively for New Southend visitors.

Walks to Rochford, Prittlewell, Milton (by now just a few scattered cottages), Eastwood and Leigh were all popular, the latter being 'one of the most beautiful walks in the neighbourhood'.

Stage coaches from London arrived daily and there was a steam packet service to the city three times a week.

Religion was also beginning to make its presence felt in the new town; a large non-conformist chapel in the High Street, at the junction with Clarence Street, was built on land given by James Heygate in 1806. There was still, however, no Anglican building in Southend and parishioners still had to travel to Prittlewell. The High Street reached all the way to the London Road by now, but beyond there were open fields.

In 1831 Southend featured in Thomas Wright's *History of the County of Essex* and the Assembly Room at the *Royal Hotel* and the theatre in the Old Town were both described as being 'fitted up in a superior style of elegance and ... well-attended in the season'.

Southend was becoming increasingly popular and in both 1833 and 1834 a young novelist, Benjamin Disraeli, later prime minister, came to visit. He stayed at Porters, then in the tenancy of Sir Francis Sykes but owned, like much of the southern central portion of Prittlewell parish, by the Heygate family.

'I can answer for Southend being very pretty,' wrote Disraeli in 1833. 'I am staying at an old grange with gable ends and antique windows ...

which is about half a mile from the town – a row of houses called a town.'

The following year he was just as enthusiastic. 'You could not have a softer climate or sunnier skies than at abused Southend. Here there are myrtles in the open air in profusion.'

**The Pier**

There were two main ways of getting to Southend – by road and by river. The latter was preferable, giving noticeably more pleasure and relaxation, though some of the vessels were cramped and slow.

Margate had seen some success with a new form of water transport, steamboats, which reduced the journey time and could carry more passengers, and by 1819 the first steamboat was tried at Southend. The difficulty with these larger ships, however, was the extensive expanse of tidal mud to be crossed if the ship arrived at low tide and passengers had to be transferred to smaller boats or onto the backs of local fishermen to be transported to the shore. The *Royal* and *Ship Hotels* maintained 'hards' that could be walked across to make this process easier and in 1802 a jetty was erected by Sir Thomas Wilson below the *Royal Hotel* to try to ease the problem, but none of these solutions was ideal.

As visitors continued to pour into the town a campaign arose to build a pier which would reach out into the tidal waters and provide direct access for passengers at all states of the tide. In the late 1820s the campaign gathered momentum, with the Heygate family, including a former Lord Mayor of London, Sir William Heygate, being the prime movers. General William Goodday Strutt, the first person of rank to live in Old Southend, was another interested party, but his concern was that his view of the river should not be spoiled by a pier in front of his house! He became a well-known local character, giving his name to 'Strutt's Parade', the stretch of the seafront in which his home, Rayleigh House, was situated (near the *Falcon*). The barge-owning Vandervoord family were also involved, though in their case it was because they wanted the pier to be built close to their business base, the *Minerva*.

Despite some opposition – among others from John Bayntun Scratton, Milton's lord of the manor, who was concerned about its effects on the oyster beds – the case for the pier steadily gained strength. By the late 1820s its construction was formally authorised and Sir William Heygate, who returned to Southend with the good news of the Pier Bill's progress through Parliament, was pulled around town in his carriage in celebration by local people who unhitched his horses and took up the shafts themselves. In 1829 the then Lord Mayor of London, Sir William Thompson, laid the foundation stone and by summer 1830 the pier was open to the public.

The Pier Act, which authorised the pier's construction, also included conditions relating to the lowering and improvement of Royal Hill, the construction of a new shore road to Shoebury and the opening up of a more direct route to

**34** Sir William Heygate, one of the leading pier proponents, pictured in 1822.

**35** A painting of Southend pier, *c.*1850, showing Pier Hill leading up to the *Royal Hotel*. The wooden pier was later replaced with an iron one.

**36**   The horse-drawn pier train, pictured *c*.1890.

Prittlewell. Progress, however, was slow and by 1835 it was apparent that not all these conditions would be fulfilled. The pier had reached around 1,500 feet in length, nowhere near enough to take it to low water, and passengers arriving at low tide still had some inconvenience to experience. Although the shore end of the journey could be made on 'dry land', visitors now had to wait on a raised wooden 'island' called The Mount (which also supported a lighthouse) until they could be boated across to a 'hard', along which they then walked to the pier. It was better than being carried on the backs of fishermen, but it was still not ideal.

Fresh powers were sought, a second Act was passed and by 1846 the pier had reached 1¼ miles in length, enough to enable embarkation at all states of the tide. Later, a horse-drawn tram was provided to carry passengers' luggage and, ultimately, the

passengers themselves. There was also a small harbour on the eastern side of the pier.

The pier made Southend even more welcoming and more and more steamers began to tie up at its end. It was now possible to go up to London on one day and return on the next and this, coupled with an ever-improving coach service, encouraged a steadily growing stream of people into the town. Nevertheless, the resident population remained small: 2,266 in 1831 (for Prittlewell, Southend and Milton combined) – a fraction of the numbers at Margate and Brighton. Ten years later it was still only 2,339, a rise of just 73 people!

Dr. A.B. Granville, who visited Southend in 1841, was in no doubt about the attractions of the town. 'The cockney,' he wrote, 'who, during the summer, stops short at Gravesend in his excursion down the Thames and is in ecstasies at that commonplace sort of retreat, can form no idea of

**37** The Tithe map of Southend for 1841, showing the extent of development of the town. Old Southend Road leads down to the seafront to the right where the Old Town is concentrated, whilst the New Town's access road — the High Street — leads direct to the London Road at the left. New and Old Southends are still separate settlements. The long straight line at the bottom is the pier.

the beauties he would enjoy were he to extend his steaming trip down the river as far as Southend.'

## A Separate Parish

Despite remaining small, Southend had nevertheless evolved considerably from its mid-18th-century origins as the South End of Prittlewell and was by now a thriving community in its own right. Nevertheless, it was still only a part of the older Prittlewell parish and parishioners still had to traipse across the fields to Prittlewell church whenever they wanted to attend a service. True, the High Street now existed and the Pier Act made provision for a direct route beyond it to the mother village, but this was still some years off.

In the early 1830s the possibility of building a church specifically for Southend was discussed and, like the campaign for the pier, it gradually gained momentum. A site was acquired on land at the top of the hill to the east of Grove Terrace – ideally situated midway between Old and New Southend – and in 1842 the new church of St John the Baptist was opened by the Bishop of London.

**38** The parish church of St John the Baptist, *c*.1900. The formation of a new ecclesiastical parish for Southend gave the town its first physical break from Prittlewell.

At the same time, Southend was formally granted separate ecclesiastical parish status; thus, one of its major ties with old Prittlewell village was severed. The Reverend George Lillingston was appointed first minister of the new parish. He remained for six years until his early death in 1848 – a tablet commemorating his life can be seen inside the church.

**39**  The Tithe map of Prittlewell from 1841. There is no Victoria Avenue and the village remains centred on West, North and East Streets at the parish church. Earls Hall and Prior's Hall manors are just north of the village, while Sutton Road to the east (right) connects it to Rochford and Southend.

## Prittlewell

While the new resort of Southend was springing up in the south-eastern corner of Prittlewell parish, life in the old village went on as it had done for centuries. Some of Southend's visitors no doubt made it to Prittlewell, as it was on the list of interesting countryside walks, but it remained a completely separate settlement.

Around 1800 a wider, more substantial bridge was built over the brook at the foot of Prittlewell Hill to accommodate increasing cart traffic and the village school also underwent expansion, being enlarged with a new schoolroom in 1817 to accommodate girls as well as boys. By the 1830s about 80 pupils were taught there.

By the time of the 1824 Southend guidebook, the Reverend Frederick Nolan was Prittlewell's incumbent. He proved to be a controversial character, antagonising parishioners by his superior attitude and opposing the proposals to erect a church in Southend on the grounds that it would adversely affect his own successors at Prittlewell. In 1840 an argument about bellringing escalated into all-out warfare. Objecting to the early hour at which the bellringers chose to practise, Nolan went into the church with a knife and cut the bellropes. This provoked physical violence and recourse to legal action on both sides; the rectory windows were broken and the bellringers heavily fined. Despite heavy criticism and an anti-Nolan effigy and song, the vicar survived the incident and remained at Prittlewell until his death in 1864 – a statistically impressive total of 42 years' service.

William White's *Directory of Essex* in 1848 described Prittlewell as 'a neat and well-built village with many modern houses'. It had a carrier service to Chelmsford from the *Spread Eagle* and a lively local business trade. It included 'the small hamlet of Milton and the handsome bathing place of Southend, the latter of which contains two-thirds of the population and has many elegant houses'. Milton itself was described as being 'a pleasant western suburb of Southend'.

## The Railway

By the early 1850s Prittlewell and Southend were both growing steadily, with well-established communities and supporting services. The roads and river continued to bring high-class visitors to the area throughout the summer months and the district was recognised as one of reputable and fashionable retreat.

That would all change, however, with the coming of the railway.

*Four*

# Expansion

**The Railway**

The railway began to make itself felt long before it arrived in Southend. The first lines in the county sprang up in the early 1840s and the main London-Colchester line brought trains as close as Brentwood. People began to travel there by rail and then by carriage to Southend, so shortening the journey.

It was not long, however, before railway companies began to look towards Southend itself for a new line, seeing the business potential of the growing resort. The town of Tilbury, some 15-20 miles upriver, was also a strategically important prize, since it was a popular port-of-call for river traffic, lying opposite the Rosherville Pleasure Gardens at Gravesend, one of the most popular steamer destinations at the time. By the early 1850s, the idea for a London, Tilbury and Southend (L.T.S.) line was born.

The railway reached what was to become Southend Central station in 1856. It was then both the end of the line and the only station in the town. (Leigh was the only other station at this time in the area covered by the modern borough – it had opened a year or so earlier as the line inched its way from Benfleet to Southend.) The original plan for Southend was for the station terminus to be on the foreshore, below Royal Terrace to the west of the pier, but residents in the Terrace voiced complaints and forced an amendment which stated that engines could not blow off steam within half a mile of their houses. This effectively killed the seafront route and the line was diverted inland at Chalkwell.

The L.T.S. Railway was a joint venture between the Eastern Counties and London & Blackwall companies. The Tilbury section was the most profitable in the early days, as trains were timetabled

**40**   Southend L.T.S. (Central) station, *c*.1881-2. The station was the end of the line until 1884.

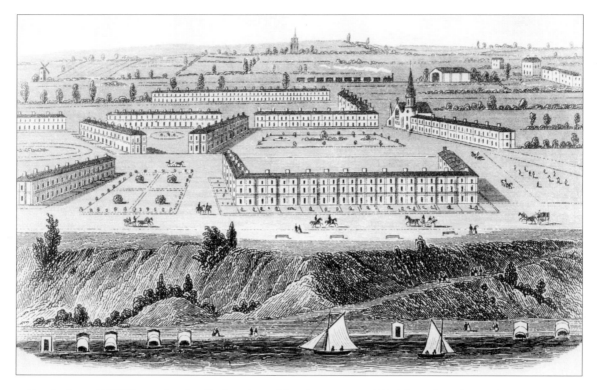

**41** A plan of Cliff Town, Southend's first planned housing estate, *c.*1850. The railway line and L.T.S. station can be seen in the background, as can a somewhat stylised Prittlewell church. The windmill at the top left is presumably at Milton at the end of Avenue Road.

to meet steamers on the river, whence passengers would take their onward journey either to Gravesend or all the way downriver to Southend. The line into Southend from Tilbury remained single-track for the first few months of operation, but this was soon doubled as rail travel became more popular. Fares were deliberately cheap to attract passengers from the river and in due course the railway led to the demise of the pleasure steamer.

The contractors for the line – Peto, Brassey and Betts – saw Southend as a place ripe for development. They bought up a large area of land on the clifftop to the west of Royal Terrace and even took over the running of the pier. The lease for the line was agreed until 1875, so they could create a lucrative business cycle, bringing people into the town in their trains, building new houses for them and seeing those houses attracting yet more people. This was the beginning of a boom period of

development for the late-Victorian town. It also marked the beginning of commuter traffic – arguably still to this day the railway's most important source of income.

The railway cut journey times to London to around an hour and a half. Those who remembered the early days of river and road transport, when several days' journey had been required, must have been amazed!

The arrival of the railway changed the face of the town forever. As one 20th-century writer would later recall somewhat poignantly about the early rail day-tripper, 'that Southend had ever been an aristocratic retreat would have seemed absurd to him, had he cared enough to read its history'. The select resort for the fashionable and wealthy was transformed overnight into a Londoners' playground, with trains providing cheap and easy access for those who could never have afforded a carriage or steamer

**42**   Nelson Terrace and Clifftown Road from an undated engraving. Nelson Terrace (left) was part of the Cliff Town estate and Southend's first purpose-built shopping street. The shop at the right-hand end of the parade still retains its original shopfront.

ride or the time away from home. The other change was that railways in general allowed more distant resorts to compete with Southend for business. Weymouth, for example, which had been too far to travel by road from London in a day, was now much more accessible. Southend's survival in the early days was to be as much from its residential development as from its tourist facilities.

## Cliff Town

The estate which really kick-started this development was called Cliff Town. It was shown on some early plans as 'Middleton New Town', perhaps an intended replacement for the nearby and largely long-lost Milton, and was Southend's first planned housing estate. Constructed *c*.1860, it was built on land to the west of the High Street and Royal Terrace, south of the railway, and was laid out symmetrically in pleasant leafy streets of attractive houses (Capel Terrace, Cashiobury Terrace, etc.), most of which afforded residents views over the estuary.

The local historian, J.W. Burrows, writing in 1909, was of the view that the estate plan was 'superior to many estate plans subsequently adopted in the Borough for extensive building operations'. Modern-day planners have recognised this and Cliff Town is now a conservation area.

The new estate included a pub, the *Railway Tavern*, and a church, Clifftown Congregational, as well as Southend's first purpose-built shopping street, Nelson Terrace, later to become Nelson Street. Though most of the shops have now been converted into offices, one original shopfront does remain, at the northern end of the western side.

## Religion

The opening of the Clifftown Congregational Church in 1865 was a visible sign that religions other than Anglican were prospering in the growing town. An 'Independent' chapel had existed in the High Street since as early as 1806 (at the corner of what would become Clarence Street) and it is said that worship had been taking place in other premises since 1799.

There was also a Congregational Chapel in Prittlewell (built in 1839), which stood, set-back,

**43**  Clifftown Congregational Church, *c*.1890s. The garden area is now a bowling green and the surrounding streets (and church) are part of a conservation area.

on the west side of North Street almost opposite the parish church.

The Anglican faith too was prospering. The mother church of St Mary the Virgin at Prittlewell was restored in 1870-1, whilst St John the Baptist at Southend, built only in 1842, was already in need of enlargement. North and south aisles were added in 1869 and a new chancel in 1873.

A Baptist Chapel was erected in East Street, Prittlewell, in 1854 (though meetings had been taking place in other premises since the 1820s) and some 20 years later Baptists took over a corrugated iron building in Hamlet Road in Southend, originally a mission hall for Anglicans, which stood just across the railway from Cliff Town's Milton Place. The iron church was later replaced by a brick building and in 1901, when the Avenue Baptist Church opened in Milton Road, it was sold back to the Church of England and became St Mark's.

The first Catholic church, St Helen's in Milton Road, appeared in 1869, whilst the Salvation Army set up a citadel in 1887 in Clarence Road. The Methodists had a chapel in Old Southend in the mid-19th century, east of the *Minerva*, on the shore side of the road, and new premises opened at Park Road in 1872. The local historian, Philip Benton, described this latter building as 'one of the greatest architectural ornaments of Southend'.

Other denominations, including the locally prominent Peculiar People, also had strong followings in the town.

### The Local Board
With the advent of the railway and the construction of Cliff Town, Southend was taking shape as a modern, independent town. Yet it was still governed administratively from Prittlewell, by now a much smaller and comparatively insignificant place.

**44** The grave of James and Anna Heygate in Prittlewell churchyard. The Heygate family was instrumental in shaping the destiny of the early Southend town.

Southend people wanted control of their own affairs and in 1866 they got their wish with the establishment of the Local Board of Health.

The Local Board was the forerunner of the modern-day council. It had full responsibility for health matters in the town (clean drinking water, good sewerage, medical treatment, etc.) and its remit gradually extended to cover such diverse items as planning, highways and education. The Board was given control of the area covered by the ecclesiastical parish of St John the Baptist – basically the bit that had been Old and New Southends plus Cliff Town and a few embryonic roads on the outskirts of the latter. Prittlewell (and the rest of the parish) continued to be run by the Prittlewell parish vestry.

The first chairman of the Southend Local Board was James Heygate, son of the James Heygate who had bought much of New Southend and brother of Sir William Heygate the pier proponent. William Gregson was appointed as their clerk. Initially,

**45** The Public Hall in Alexandra Street, c.1872. This was the home of the Local Board, which was responsible for the early administration of Southend.

**46**   The junction of Queens Road and Princes Street, pictured in 1924. This area was developed in the late 19th century and connected the High Street to the Park Estate.

meetings were held at the *Royal Hotel*, but in 1872 a new Public Hall was opened in Alexandra Street (built to connect the High Street to Cliff Town's Alexandra Road) and the Board took up offices there.

Early issues for the Local Board included sewerage, planning permissions for housebuilding and the making up of roads. As in other communities at this period, the question of sewerage proved a particularly taxing one, with only the new Cliff Town Estate relatively well provided for. The majority of Southend's sewage, like that in many coastal towns, was simply discharged into the sea. All new houses were under strict scrutiny.

Some of the earliest planning issues related to the housing estates that would follow Cliff Town. Across the railway from Milton Place the Park Estate was being created (around Hamlet Road, Park Road and Avenue Road). This was erected in the early 1870s.

The Park Estate is of particular historic interest since it takes its name from Southend Park, a recreational area used briefly for cricket and cycling which stood approximately between Park Crescent and Park Terrace. When the park was first opened it stood in an undeveloped area of the town. The first houses grew up facing the park and later the parkland itself was built on. The difference in housing styles can still be seen. Apart from the 'Park' street-names, two pubs survive on the London Road as reminders of this lost recreational area – the *Park Tavern* and the *Cricketers* inn.

These areas of land had come onto the market in 1869 after the decision by the last lord of the manors of Milton and Priors Hall, Daniel Robert Scratton, to sell up and move to Devon. Land between Royal Terrace and the railway (between the High Street and Cliff Town) and the whole area between High Street and Avenue Road, south of London Road, was earmarked for development. Much of this land was bought by Thomas Dowsett (a later mayor of the town (see below)) and J.G. Baxter, who then sold it for building.

**47**   Southend Gas Company employees, *c*.1905.

Milton Hall passed ultimately to the Sisters of Nazareth as a care home for children and the elderly. Prittlewell Priory, for the time being, remained in private ownership.

Another new estate at this time was Porters Town, which stood to the north-west of Porters Grange, west of Sutton Road and north of Southchurch Road. This comprised a series of grid-like streets – Milton Street, Sutton Street, Coleman Street, etc. – which had been built on land from the old Porters estate. The estate had been sold off in lots in 1868, the Grange itself being purchased by Local Board chairman, James Heygate.

Porters Town soon became a separate parish, served by its own church, All Saints, built in 1877. Benton recalls that boundary stones bearing the legend 'Prittlewell All Saints District' were laid out at strategic points. The Heygate family, notably Miss E.A. Heygate, were great supporters of the new church.

Southend's infrastructure was also beginning to take shape. Southend Gas Company was formed in 1854, and the supply of gas from works on land to the east of Old Southend started the following year. Gas-holders became a feature of the Lower Town's skyline and gaslamps began to appear in the town's streets. The gasworks moved from the seafront in the late 1950s/early 1960s – the site they occupied is still awaiting redevelopment.

Water supply was another major concern for any growing Victorian town and in Southend as elsewhere the arrival of the railway, which needed copious amounts of water for its steam engines, helped with the establishment of a good, reliable supply as a replacement for the ditches and wells which had hitherto supplied local people. Southend Waterworks was established in Milton Road, just north of the railway bridge, in the late 1850s. A covered reservoir nearby in Cambridge Road soon became a well-known local feature.

As the Board's responsibilities grew, so did its workload. In 1875 it was increased to nine members.

**48**   Southend Waterworks (on the left) in 1923. The bridge carries Milton Road over the railway line and Cambridge Road disappears to the right in the foreground. The big building in the centre background is St Bernard's school.

## Education

One of the principal topics of interest to Victorian Southend was education.

The first proper all-inclusive school in the town was the National School in Old Southend, established by public subscription in 1855 opposite the *Britannia* pub. This was governed by trustees, including the lord of the manor and the rector of St John the Baptist. In time, however, the management of the school fell into disrepute and the number of places available for the growing number of children also became inadequate. With financial problems, too, the school temporarily closed.

The Congregational Church also ran a school in the High Street, known as the 'British School' and operating since at least the early 1840s. It stood close to the original 1806 chapel and was set up initially for the education of non-Church of England

pupils. It was coping with the workload, but it too was showing signs of strain.

In 1876 the national Board of Education instructed local people to do something about inadequate schooling in the town. After some disagreements about the best approach, a Prittlewell School Board was formed in 1877 under the chairmanship of Prittlewell rector, the Reverend Spencer Wigram. Wigram had first-hand knowledge of local schools since during his incumbency the original 18th-century Prittlewell school had moved from its position at the bottom of Prittlewell Hill to a new site in East Street, just east of the church. The rector, along with the Heygate and Scratton families, had personally met much of the cost of its relocation.

Amongst the first recommendations of the new School Board was the construction of a new

**49**  The 1st Edition Ordnance Survey map of Southend for 1873. Southend has been growing steadily since the Tithe map, and Cliff Town and the other new estates have begun to appear. There has been little further development of the Old Town, though a new pub, the *Castle*, has replaced the Caroline Baths (where the Sea Life Centre would be later). The seafront in this area has not yet lost its greens.

Most of the new development is westwards from the New Town towards the old Milton hamlet. Just to the north of central Southend the embryonic Porters Town is appearing, the only significant new development north of the London Road.

Southend and Prittlewell are still quite distinct settlements, although next to Porters Town a start has been made on the proposed link road between the two. This would later become Victoria Avenue. Perhaps the most surprising thing is how rural the area is – and only 125 years ago!

'London Road' school (some distance west of the London Road's junction with the High Street), which opened in 1879 and was able to accommodate 500 pupils. The British School closed its doors for the last time.

## Police

With a growing town and a high influx of day-trippers, the question of policing began to take some prominence. The modern police force had its origins *c.*1840, when the old system of parish constables was superseded by the first full-time regular police forces. Southend originally came under the jurisdiction of the Prittlewell parish constable, but within 30 years of the establishment of the new county-wide force, the town was being served by its own local officers. In 1873 the force decided to build a new police station near the Public Hall in Alexandra Street, a move which was to give the town for the first time a senior police presence under Inspector, later Superintendent, Samuel Hawtree. As the Local Board's offices were also in Alexandra Street and a courthouse was provided next door to the new police station, the thoroughfare soon became the 'civic centre' of the growing town.

**50** Eastern Esplanade in 1908, showing the Methodist Church (the double-roofed building, centre left) and the National School (right). The workmen are laying tramlines (see pp.60–3).

**51** The Southend Fire Brigade in 1878.

## Fire

Fire prevention, too, was becoming an issue and in 1875 the Local Board began to consider setting up a voluntary fire brigade for Southend. In 1877 they purchased a second-hand pump (horse-drawn then, of course) and rented premises for it in Market Place, a narrow alleyway off Alexandra Street. Volunteers were appointed in October and had to deal with their first major fire in March 1878 when a High Street shop went up in flames. The Brigade was led in the early days by Captain G. Lingwood, who had useful connections with the Southend Waterworks Company!

## Take-over of Prittlewell

By 1877 the comparative importance of Southend and Prittlewell was such that the national Local Government Board recommended the take-over of the Prittlewell parish vestry by the Southend Local Board. This was duly accomplished and it meant that the Local Board now controlled the whole of Prittlewell parish, not just the Southend part of it. The ancient estates of Milton, Chalkwell, Porters and others came within its jurisdiction. Membership of the Local Board was increased to 12, the three new members representing Prittlewell. The first signs of later electoral wards were beginning to appear.

This take-over – just 11 years after Southend had gained administrative independence from Prittlewell and just 35 years after any sort of break (with the formation of St John the Baptist's ecclesiastical parish) – was to prove the first in a long line of take-overs up to the 1930s. The modern Southend upstart now controlled the whole of the ancient Prittlewell parish and it would not be long before it set its sights on other neighbouring parishes.

## Building Boom

The 1870s and 1880s were the boom period for building in Victorian Southend. The Park and Porters Town Estates significantly increased the developed area, the railway brought more and more people and the administrative merger of Southend and Prittlewell made people think of the possibilities of building between the two towns.

The High Street area to the north of the railway was gradually being built on and the thoroughfare rapidly became Southend's principal shopping street in preference to Cliff Town's Nelson Terrace (Street). The northern end of the High Street, originally blocked by the 'White Gates' at the London Road to all without permission to use it, was known for a time as Whitegate Road before that name was transferred to a new street nearby.

Development of the area around Queen's Road between the northern part of the High Street and the Park Estate to the west began and Warrior Square also appeared. The Clarence Street and York Road areas were also developed, the latter being considerably extended eastwards to link with the growing housing areas at Pleasant Row and Old Southend Road (by now called Brewery Road in part, following the establishment of a brewery there c.1850). Beyond the latter, the 400-year-old Thames Farm was eventually sold for development. Its old entrance would soon be realigned to form a new road, Woodgrange Drive. The brewery later moved to the High Street under the name 'Middleton Brewery' and then 'Luker's Brewery' after its owner, Henry Luker. The brewery stood where the old Odeon cinema is now and its owner is commemorated there in 'Luker Road'. The adjacent *Middleton Hotel* evolved into what is now *O'Neills*. The *London Tavern* also appeared just across the High Street from Clifftown Road, and, further south, the *Pier Hotel* opened in Grove Terrace.

To the east of the town, more buildings began to straggle along the seafront towards Southchurch, while to the west there were plans for a 'high-class suburban retreat' in the old Milton/Hamlet area, between Milton Road and Hamlet Court Road. This area, at the far end of the cliffs to the west of Southend, soon gained the name 'Westcliff' and, as time went on, old Milton lost its identity and the new name came into everyday use.

The Local Board's management had given the town's development some structural order and its principal businessmen and community leaders were also beginning to emerge. The infrastructure – gas, water, sewerage – was well developed and facilities were extended to Prittlewell following the latter's take-over. Streets were being made up and the never-ending influx of visitors and a growing resident population led to the establishment of more shops and services, including a bank and a Post Office. The town also had its own newspaper, the *Southend Standard*, established in 1873.

Brickfields began to spring up all over the town, causing much consternation for Benton.

'The brickfields … which are extending, are not an attractive feature,' he wrote at this time, 'and much of the neighbourhood has lost its rural character. The widening of the Hamlet lanes, the destruction of the woods and groves … excite regret.'

Southend slowly but surely began to expand outwards. From now on, there would be no looking back.

## Railway Extension

By the early 1880s the L.T.S. railway company was considering plans for extending its line eastwards from Southend to Shoeburyness. This would take trains through Southchurch parish and into the remotest parts of the peninsula which hitherto had remained largely agricultural. The only establishment of any note in the region was a military one at South Shoebury which had been established in 1849. Soldiers – and their heavy equipment – would no doubt benefit from a new line …

The Local Board expressed some opposition to the proposal, fearing it would lead to the creation of a new resort in Shoeburyness and open up competition between the two settlements. Nevertheless, the railway company got its way and in 1882 an Act was passed to enable both the construction of the Shoeburyness extension and the provision of a new more direct line between Barking and Pitsea, which would cut journey times and save Southend passengers from the 'Tilbury loop'.

The first effect of the new line was at the station. The stationmaster's house, which stood in the High Street to the immediate east of the station building, was in the direct line of the planned new route and was duly demolished. A dilemma for the builders was at what level the line should cross the High Street. They eventually chose to cross over it, principally through fears that trains passing underneath a raised road could frighten traders' horses and because a level-crossing would be too much of an inconvenience to High Street business. The railway bridge is now one of the High Street's most significant landmarks.

The line to Shoebury opened on 1 February 1884. Apart from passengers, it also carried growing freight traffic and its arrival sowed the seeds for opening up the area for brickfields and subsequent housing development.

The shorter route to the town between Barking and Pitsea was opened in 1888.

On the 1887 August bank holiday, some 25,000 people visited Southend. High on revelry, many of them missed their trains back to London and there was a mass sleep-out in the town.

## Victoria Avenue

The growing facilities in Southend and the centralisation of administration there led to renewed calls for a direct road link between the town and Prittlewell village. A start had been made on one by the time of the 1873 Ordnance Survey map, but it had not got very far.

By the late 1880s work was properly under way and on 1 June 1889 the new road – Victoria Avenue – was formally opened. It entered Prittlewell at the junction with North, East and West Streets, forming a crossroads outside the church. The old *Blue Boar* pub, which stood in the way of the new road, had to be demolished and was rebuilt slightly to the west, where it now stands.

The Southend end of the road began at the top of the High Street, forming a crossroads there with the High Street and London and Southchurch Roads. This crossroads, later a roundabout, would soon become one of the main focal points of the town as 'Victoria Circus'.

## Victoria Hospital

Since the early days of the Local Board there had been concerns about the provision of good health facilities in the town. By the time of Queen Victoria's Golden Jubilee in 1887 it was decided to commemorate the occasion by building a hospital. A committee was set up under the chairmanship of former Local Board member, Dr. Warwick, with William Gregson acting as secretary.

Things moved quickly. In January 1887 a public meeting was held to launch a fundraising appeal and by summer sufficient money had been raised to purchase half an acre of land at the south-eastern corner of Warrior Square. It was decided to call it

**52** Southend Victoria Hospital, which stood in Warrior Square roughly where the swimming pool is now, was established to celebrate Queen Victoria's Golden Jubilee in 1887.

the Southend Victoria Hospital in recognition of the Queen's Jubilee and in August Lady Brooke laid the foundation stone. The building was formally opened on 30 May 1888 by Mrs. Carne Rasch, wife of the local MP. It held just eight beds, but it was a start. It was also a far cry from the remote 'pesthouses' or isolation hospitals to which sick people had historically been sent to keep them away from the rest of the population.

**Parish Burial Ground**

Provision was also made for those whom medicine could not save. Deceased Prittlewell villagers hitherto were interred in the churchyard at St Mary the Virgin, whilst more recently Southend people were laid to rest in the churchyard of St John the Baptist.

**53** The now-overgrown chapel and surrounding Prittlewell parish burial ground in North Road, which opened for interments in April 1881.

**54**   A rare picture of the Committee and Stewards at the opening of the G.E.R. line to Southend (Victoria station) on 1 October 1889. The station building can be seen in the background.

By the late 1860s space at St Mary's was at a premium and the vicar, the Reverend Wigram, asked the Local Board for a new Parish Burial Ground. It was 1880 (by which time Wigram had been succeeded by Thomas Osmotherley Reay) before it appeared. The site chosen was in North Road, just north of Milton Hall, and it opened in April 1881. St Mary's stopped accepting admissions shortly afterwards.

**A New Line**

With rail travel a growth area and Southend already proven as a growth town, the L.T.S.'s principal rival, the Great Eastern Railway (G.E.R.), began to show an interest. It owned the main London-Colchester line and was keen to create a Southend branch from that.

By 1887 the route had been chosen and the construction of the line, starting at Shenfield, was under way. It took two years to reach Southend: the formal opening took place there on 1 October 1889. As with the L.T.S. line, the track was initially single and was not completely doubled this side of Wickford until early in the following century.

The arrival of the G.E.R. was undoubtedly a bonus for Southend people. The Local Board

described it as 'extremely beneficial' and the *Southend Standard* said it would make Southend townsfolk feel more in contact with the rest of Essex. Those in the main town now had a choice of lines, whilst the inhabitants of Prittlewell no longer had to make the journey to Southend – they had their own station. It was built at the eastern end of East Street, underneath which the line now passed. Southend's new station was located in Victoria Avenue, in the space between the Avenue itself and Milton Street.

Since they were run by different companies, the two Southend stations would be known for some time afterwards by the names of the lines' owners, the L.T.S., later L.M.S. (now Southend Central), and the G.E.R., later L.N.E.R. (now Southend Victoria).

**A New Pier**

Southend had changed significantly since the pier had been erected in 1830. The structure was now well over 50 years old and beginning to show its age, the buildings at the entrance looking tatty and unsightly. Since 1875 it had been owned by the Local Board and in 1884 the Board decided on a brand new pier and tollhouse entrance to meet the

**55**   The new iron pier and tollhouse, *c.*1893.

needs of the modern town. The decision drew some opposition, no doubt through fears that the pier's upkeep costs would adversely affect the rates, and there was some disagreement about a high-level approach (from Royal (Pier) Hill) or a low-level one (from the beach). The high-level option was ultimately chosen, as the Board had plans for a new road under the pier and on to the west below the Shrubbery.

The new high-level brick tollhouse was erected in 1885, though the replacement pier (requiring an Act of Parliament) was not completed until 1889. The new pier, designed by Sir James Brunlees, was a sturdy iron construction, replacing the original wooden one and ultimately extending even further

out into the estuary than its predecessor. The opportunity was taken to replace the old horse-drawn carriages with a brand new electric railway, the first of its kind on a pleasure pier. This was unveiled in 1890, with distinctive open-sided carriages which soon acquired the nickname of 'toastrack'. The old 'Octagon' entertainments marquee at the landward end (through which the horse-drawn trams had passed even when performances were on!) was also replaced, in this case with a permanent pavilion. The Board's new 'under pier' road was also constructed, becoming the first section of Western Esplanade. Benton wrote at the time that the Board's decision to purchase the pier 'seems destined to prove a very wise and lucrative transaction'.

**56** Southend pier, *c.*1890, showing the new electric pier trains.

A short loading pier, which had stood next to the wooden pleasure pier (on the east side next to the harbour), was moved downriver to the vicinity of the *Minerva* public house when the iron pier opened.

1879 had seen the first lifeboat station for Southend, with a boat called somewhat fancifully *The Boys of England and Edwin J. Brett* (named after its principal financial supporters). *The Boys…* and its early successors, *Theodore and Herbert* and *James Stevens No.9*, proved a boon to local sea safety.

The Alexandra Yacht Club started around this time and was instrumental in getting various national yacht races to start from Southend's pier. One of these, in 1887, the year of Queen Victoria's Golden Jubilee, even attracted the Prince of Wales.

One of the most colourful characters in this period of the pier's history was William Bradley – piermaster, pierhead lightkeeper and sometime coxswain of the Southend lifeboat. In addition to his formal pier duties, Bradley saved many lives by diving from the pier to help people in distress in the waters below. He received public recognition for his services and was later elected a councillor and alderman.

### The Town Council

By the late 1880s thought was being given to replacing the Local Board with a Town Council, which would have wider powers and enable local people to have better control over their own affairs. In September 1888 it was formally proposed and

by December the Local Board had collectively resolved to recommend it. Thus began a lot of hard work and growing excitement as the town looked forward to gaining a Charter of Incorporation and the increased powers and independence that came with it.

Much of the work towards this was done outside the Local Board. The Board itself carried on with its usual business for another four years until incorporation was granted. Its last chairman, John H. Burrows, proprietor of the *Southend Standard*, was one of a select band of Local Board members who went on to serve on the new Council. He gave many years' service in the fields of education and health and also served as a magistrate and a County Councillor.

The last Local Board meeting was held on 5 November 1892. A formal vote of thanks was recorded in the minutes for John H. Burrows and the long-serving clerk, William Gregson. Much had happened since the Local Board's inception and those who had served on it had much to be pleased with.

The Charter of Incorporation was granted in August 1892 and the Charter document formally received on 19 September 1892, celebrated as 'Charter Day'. The Lord Mayor of London, Sir David Evans, visited and there was a procession through the town and fireworks on the cliffs. Children were given a commemorative medal.

A new era in the town's history had begun.

# Five

# The Town Council

The years presided over by the Town Council – also referred to as the Municipal Borough Council and the Corporation – were arguably the most important in Southend's history. From 1892 (when their work commenced) to 1914 (when the town achieved County Borough status) the councillors who ran the town laid down the foundations for virtually everything that was to come. As Prittlewell curate Thomas Archer had predicted, streets began to extend across the length and breadth of the old Prittlewell parish and beyond. The shape of today's town – its housing, its network of roads and all its infrastructure – was largely defined during this intensive period of development.

## The Town Council

The first meeting of the new Town Council took place on 9 November 1892 at the Southend Institute buildings in Clarence Road. Eighteen councillors were elected, representing three electoral wards – West Ward, East Ward and North (or Prittlewell) Ward. They included many who had served on the Local Board.

Their first task was to elect a Mayor – someone who would preside over Council meetings as the Chairman had done on the old Local Board and be the public face of the Council in the town and beyond. They chose Thomas Dowsett.

Dowsett was a native of Prittlewell and had been elected to represent that ward. He had worked his way from humble beginnings to own a variety of businesses, perhaps the most profitable being his Southend-on-Sea Estates Company. In partnership with J.G. Baxter, the Ingram family and others, he went on to own much land and property in the town. He was active in church (mainly at Clifftown Congregational) and had served on the Local Board.

**57** Thomas Dowsett, the town's first mayor, in 1892. Dowsett is sitting in the mayoral chair, which was made from one of the piles of the old wooden pier. It now resides in Porters, the mayor's civic home.

He had vision for the future and was never afraid to invest his own money in the interests of the town. Southend Victoria Hospital, schools and the poor all benefited. Almshouses established by Dowsett in Chelmsford Avenue survive to this day. He retired

**58** Marine Parade in 1911. Between the turn-of-the-century and the First World War Marine Parade and Eastern and Western Esplanades were laid out, made up and widened. This picture captures some of the work in progress.

from the Council in 1898 and died in 1906, being buried in the churchyard of St John the Baptist, the final resting place of many of his contemporaries. Dowsett Avenue, a road named after him linking London Road and Victoria Avenue, existed until town centre redevelopment in the late 1960s.

John H. Burrows was appointed Deputy Mayor and William Gregson, long-serving Clerk to the Local Board, was chosen as Town Clerk.

The local MP, Major Frederick Carne Rasch, presented at the first meeting a silver mace for use by the Mayor, and in February 1893 Dowsett presented the chain of office which is still used by Southend mayors to this day. Six months later a local architect, Edward Wright, presented a commemorative chair for the Mayor which was made from one of the oak timbers from the old wooden pier. This chair is also still in use, not least for the Mayor's official photograph.

The first seven committees were set up on 23 November 1892. They give a good indication of what was most important to the town – health, highways, buildings, pier, licensing, finance and parliamentary (the latter dealt with legislation issues).

Dowsett was followed as Mayor by Daniel Wright Gosset (1893-4), John Rumbelow Brightwell (1894-5), Alfred Prevost (1895-6), Bernard Wilshire Tolhurst (1896-7), John H. Burrows (1897-8), Frederick Francis Ramuz (1898-1900) and Joseph Francis (1900-1). The names of Brightwell and Ramuz are remembered today in Southend street-names. Tolhurst was in office at the time of Queen Victoria's Diamond Jubilee in June 1897 and it was he who gave the town the famous white statue of the Queen which stands on the cliffs in Clifftown Parade. It was formally unveiled on 24 May 1898. Ramuz, Tolhurst and four-times Mayor, James Colbert Ingram, were all major developers in the town.

**59**   Western Esplanade (known at this point as The Leas) in 1904 during widening and making-up operations.

The Mayor was supported by six aldermen, generally the most experienced and respected councillors, chosen by the councillors themselves from their own number. Aldermen did not have to face public elections during their period of office, but there was always a by-election in a ward for a replacement councillor whenever anyone was made an alderman. There were therefore effectively 18 councillors (elected by the people) and six aldermen (chosen from the elected councillors by the councillors themselves) governing the town.

The Council also at this time adopted its own coat of arms, bearing the legend *Forti Nihil Difficile* ('To the brave, nothing is difficult'). Frequently criticised for being unheraldic, it was later replaced.

In June 1893 the Council took the decision formally to change the name of the town – in the hope of increasing its appeal as a resort – to 'Southend-on-Sea'.

**The Early Years of the Town Council**

The vision and foresight shown by the Local Board was matched by the new Town Council.

The sewerage problem lingered on, but councillors cracked it with Eastern and Western Valley sewerage schemes on either side of the town, supported by a separate scheme for Prittlewell, where the land drained away to the north instead of south. This was enhanced in 1909 by the construction of a new sewage treatment works in the north of the parish, built to counter the damage to the shellfish industry caused by the discharge of untreated sewage into the sea. The sewage works still exist in this location.

In conjunction with Southend Gas Company and Southend Waterworks councillors ensured that services were connected to all properties in the town and, when electricity became available, they embraced that as well. Housing estates grew up all over the old Prittlewell parish (now Southend Borough), extending to the west as far as the Leigh boundary.

**60** Eastern Esplanade in 1908, heading towards the *Halfway House*, pictured during widening operations.

**61** Southend's cliff lift, an often overlooked attraction, which began life in the late 19th century to connect Clifton Terrace with Western Esplanade below. This particular lift dates from 1912.

On the seafront, they continued the Local Board's policy of buying up the various 'Greens' which stood opposite and to the east of the *Minerva* (Fairhead's, Pawley's, Darlow's and *Britannia*), bringing them all into Council ownership. They took steps to improve Marine Parade (widening it considerably) and to construct roads to the east and west along the shore. Between 1899 and the First World War, these roads were laid out, widened, extended and properly made up into broad attractive thoroughfares as (eventually) Eastern and Western Esplanades. As early as 1896 the Council was also considering a 'Cliff Lift' to connect Clifftown Parade with the beach below, though this took a few more years to become a reality.

**Westcliff and Chalkwell**
It was during this period that two new communities began to take shape.

**62** Hamlet Court Road in Westcliff in 1907. Named after Milton hamlet and a building called Hamlet Court, it was always an important road in the area and soon became established as Westcliff's main shopping street.

The first, Westcliff, had already been developing under the old Local Board, but now it positively blossomed into a distinct, self-sufficient community. It completely took over the area covered historically by Milton and came to centre on Hamlet Court Road, still today its principal shopping thoroughfare.

The growth of Westcliff had been accelerated by the opening of the Barking-Pitsea section of the L.T.S. railway and in the early 1890s it was agreed

that the area should have its own station. Early suggestions for this to be named 'The Hamlet' or even 'Kensington-on-Sea' were rejected and the name 'Westcliff-on-Sea' was eventually chosen. It opened in 1895.

Just as happened at Southend, the provision of a railway station led to significant growth and Westcliff soon expanded into a sizeable, and somewhat select, suburb.

**63** Westborough Road, one of the new residential streets in the Westcliff district, taken in 1908 from its junction with West Road.

**64** Ramuz Drive, Westcliff, in 1908, looking north towards Fairfax Drive and Prittle Brook, with the slope leading up to Prittlewell Chase beyond. This picture gives a good indication of the extent of the development of the town at this time.

**65** The developing western end of Southend. This is the London Road between Westcliff and Chalkwell in 1910 at its junction with Crowstone Road. Sale boards proliferate on as yet undeveloped land. The area would soon be covered with shops, as has already happened on the other side of the road.

**66** Chalkwell Esplanade in 1903, showing the Crowstone on its side in the foreground. As with Western and Eastern Esplanades, the road here is being laid out and various piles of rubble can be seen. In the middle of the picture can be seen a trail of steam from a passing steam train, whilst in the background houses disappear up the hill into the distance.

Further west, at the extreme western end of the Borough, was the Chalkwell Hall estate. As development extended from the centre of Southend this too became earmarked for housing.

In 1901 the Council struck a deal with the Chalkwell Hall Syndicate for ownership of the foreshore of the estate and also purchased Chalkwell Hall and the surrounding grounds for use as a public park. Chalkwell Esplanade and Avenue were built shortly afterwards and another new suburb – Chalkwell – quickly became established.

**Space at a Premium**
Population growth in Southend during the 19th century had been phenomenal. In 1801 Prittlewell parish (including Southend and Milton) had been

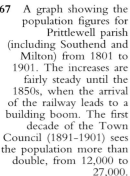

**67** A graph showing the population figures for Prittlewell parish (including Southend and Milton) from 1801 to 1901. The increases are fairly steady until the 1850s, when the arrival of the railway leads to a building boom. The first decade of the Town Council (1891-1901) sees the population more than double, from 12,000 to 27,000.

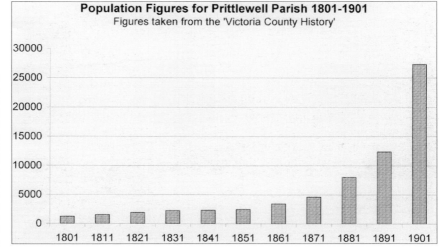

**68** Holy Trinity Church, Southchurch, *c*.1908. The picture shows the building before the enlargement which was required to serve the growing parish following Southchurch's acquisition by Southend.

home to 1,213 souls. In 1851, before the railway came, the figure was still only 2,462. Forty years later, after the boom period of the 1870s and 1880s, it had reached an incredible 12,000. By 1901, after a decade of development under the new Town Council, it was over 27,000! By 1913 development had reached Grand Drive, Chalkwell Park Drive and Recreation Avenue. Although to modern eyes these are generally thought of as Leigh streets, they actually marked the extreme western boundary of what had been Prittlewell parish.

As the town grew and the lands of old Prittlewell began to fill, councillors became even more aware of the growing burden on them to provide homes and services for an ever-increasing number of residents. With a finite amount of land in the Borough, they had to look elsewhere.

Southend had been growing rapidly since the 1850s, but until 1897 it stayed within the boundaries of the old Prittlewell parish. Now, for the first time, the net had to be cast wider as councillors thought of bringing other parishes into the Borough. The obvious choice was Southchurch.

## Southchurch

There had already been some encroachment into Southchurch parish by Southend, most notably along

the seafront road to the east of the *Minerva*. This was not surprising, since the town had begun in this vicinity, although hitherto most of the expansion had been westwards. Southend Gasworks was hard up against Southchurch's boundary and, further north, buildings had begun to reach eastwards from Porters along Southchurch Road, but the parish itself was still almost entirely agricultural. A major consideration for the choice was that sewers for the north-east part of Southend could not be drained direct to the sea without going through Southchurch parish.

Southchurch's centre was a small group of buildings around the parish church (Holy Trinity), including the *White Horse* pub, the Post Office (which stood opposite the church and was demolished *c*.1913) and the parish's own National School (now the Thorpe Bay Bridge Club). Elsewhere the only buildings were isolated farms.

Like Milton, Southchurch was originally under the ownership of Canterbury monks, who appear to have held it from at least A.D. 823 until the Dissolution (1539). (The grant of A.D. 823 was made by a man called Leofstan, whose name survives in 'Lifstan Way'.) Though in the monks' ownership, much of the land was farmed from the mid-12th to the mid-14th centuries by the

**69** The *White Horse*, Southchurch — one of the main buildings at the heart of the Southchurch community. This photograph was taken in 1914.

prominent de Southchurch family, who built the Southchurch Hall manor house and the chapel that became Southchurch parish church. Sir Richard de Southchurch (the third) was Sheriff of Essex and Hertfordshire 1265-7 (and also perhaps *c*.1272) and from 1279 to 1283 he was the King's Steward of the Liberty of Rochford. His son, Sir Peter, was appointed Justice over the King's officers in 1300. Both men were actively involved in battles on the King's behalf and Sir Peter may even have died while on active service.

The family's manor house, Southchurch Hall, now a museum, has survived as the oldest complete secular building in the modern Southend Borough. It is thought to date from at least the early 14th century (with subsequent alterations) and is an excellent example of a moated manor house of that period. The grounds, once home to outbuildings and

**70** Southchurch Hall — the original manor house for Southchurch and one of the oldest surviving secular buildings in the modern Southend Borough.

orchards, have been turned into public gardens and the now-segmented moat survives as ponds for wildfowl. There is a tradition that Southchurch Hall was

**71**  Thorpe Hall from a painting, *c*.1861. The Hall has been much altered and is currently home to Thorpe Hall Golf Club.

ransacked by rebels during the 1381 Peasants' Revolt, but there is no firm evidence for this.

At the Dissolution the manor of Southchurch Hall passed, like much of Prittlewell, to Richard, Lord Rich. It was then leased to tenant farmers until *c*.1650 when it was sub-divided into two separate manors, Southchurch Hall and Southchurch Wick.

Two other manors in Southchurch parish also existed – North Thorpe and (South) Thorpe, which may once have been Danish settlements. These were outside the ownership of the Canterbury monks at Domesday Book and were later united as 'Thorpe Hall'. A later manor house for this area still stands as the clubhouse of Thorpe Hall Golf Club (established in 1907). It carries the date '1668'.

Holy Trinity church, whose geographical location as the southernmost church in the old Rochford Hundred administrative area gave 'South Church' its name, was built in the mid-12th century. It retains many original features, including the Norman doorways and windows. Indeed it survived almost completely unaltered (other than a 17th-century timber belfry) until 1906, when massive population expansion in the parish led to the addition of a new north aisle (now the nave, the old church becoming the south aisle). This, and a subsequent addition in 1931, completely dwarf the original building.

Perhaps not surprisingly, there was some opposition in Southchurch to the take-over (though several in the Southchurch Beach area had indicated

that they were in favour). Parishioners had seen their larger neighbour grow from 2,000 to 12,000 inhabitants in barely fifty years. Their own population in 1891 was just over 900. The historic community of Prittlewell was already being swallowed up – surely the same would happen to them?

One of the principal bones of contention was the difference in rates – lower in Southchurch than in Southend. The objections were eventually overcome, but only with the concession of continued lower rates for parts of Southchurch parish.

Southchurch was formally included in Southend Borough with effect from 1 November 1897.

The take-over meant that more land was open for development. It also increased the length of coast under the Council's control to around five miles and in due course this would enable the development of a completely new resort suburb a little further to the east.

### A New Form of Transport

Over time, Southchurch began to benefit from all the improved services that went with new housing – sewerage, water, gas and electricity. Perhaps the most unexpected bonus, however, was in transport.

The Light Railways Act of 1896 had made it possible for local authorities to consider the introduction of trams in their towns. Southend was an early advocate of this new form of transport, no doubt encouraged by the success of the electric pier trains, and quickly took steps to introduce it. Trams,

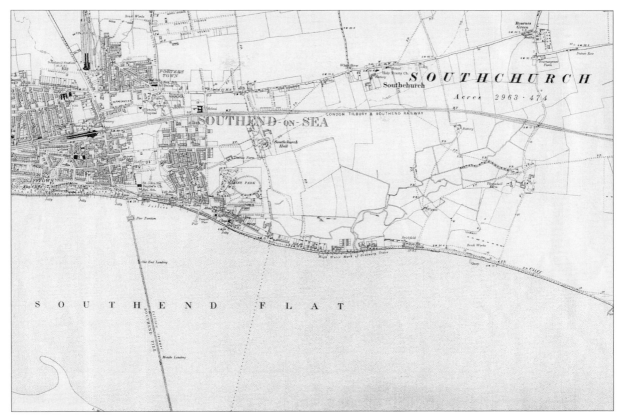

**72**   An extract from the 2nd Edition Ordnance Survey map of 1898, the year after the take-over of Southchurch by Southend. Southchurch, with its satellite settlements of Bournes Green and Thorpe Hall, is much smaller than its rapidly growing western neighbour.

of course, went hand-in-hand with electricity and, as the tramway network grew, so did the use of electricity in streets, homes and businesses.

The first tramway routes included: Southend High Street (*Middleton Hotel* terminus, north of the railway bridge) to Prittlewell (*Blue Boar*); the *Blue Boar* via West Street and North Road to the *Cricketers*; Southend High Street to Southchurch (Holy Trinity Church); and a branch line from the latter route down the former Brewery Road (Southchurch Avenue) to the *Minerva* (and therefore the seafront).

The plans also included a route from Southend High Street to Leigh (St Clement's church) which extended beyond the Borough boundary. Fortunately, however, the authority into whose territory the line was to extend, Leigh Urban District Council, was in favour of the scheme.

In central Southend the routes converged at Victoria Circus. A web of overhead tram wires crossed in all directions and it soon gained the nickname of 'Cobweb Corner'. A tramway ticket office was built in the middle of the roundabout there in 1910.

The tramway depot and electricity generating station were constructed several hundred yards to the west along London Road on the site now occupied by Sainsbury's Homebase. A bus garage was later built in front of the depot – this has recently been replaced by a new Curry's store. There is still a generating station on the site.

The first trams ran on 19 July 1901. They were immediately popular and their success prompted the Council to consider several ambitious routes – to Shoebury, Wakering, Rochford and Hadleigh.

**73** Southchurch Boulevard under construction in 1913. To build a wide dual carriageway road with a central reservation for trams through virgin countryside from Southchurch to Bournes Green was a bold step by Southend Council.

None of these was developed, however, as indecision and escalating costs put paid to most of the more extravagant ideas.

In 1908 the Council opened its first seafront service, from the *Minerva* to Bryant Avenue and back. This was extended in 1909 to the *Halfway House* pub, so named for its situation halfway between Southend and Shoebury, the next administrative area beyond Southchurch to the east. A further extension, from the *Halfway House* to 'Thorpe Hall Corner', at the bottom of the lane leading north to Thorpe Hall, was opened in 1912.

Perhaps the Council's most ambitious scheme was a circular 'tour' which ran north from the *Minerva* up Southchurch Avenue, east along Southchurch Road to the *White Horse* and beyond into the countryside as far as Bournes Green and then south down the narrow Thorpe Hall Lane to the seafront and back to the *Minerva* again. The

scheme involved the construction of two new broad, picturesque, shrub-planted, dual-carriageway roads (Southchurch Boulevard and Thorpe Hall Avenue), the widening of the railway bridge over Thorpe Hall Lane/Avenue and the construction of a new seafront road and seawall from the new Avenue to the *Minerva*. The trams would run down the central reservation, while horse (and early motor) traffic used the roads. The Council showed much foresight here in building wide thoroughfares that would later have to accommodate considerably higher traffic levels. The author of *The Tramways of South-end-on-Sea*, V.E. Burrows, described the move as 'bold and sensible planning'.

The full circular route came into operation in summer 1914 and proved immediately popular with tourists, but the high cost of the construction work was to prove a millstone round the tramway's neck for many years to come.

**74** Widening the railway bridge at Thorpe Hall Avenue in 1914. This was required as the old Thorpe Hall Lane was expanded to boulevard proportions to complete Southchurch's tramway circuit. Expenses incurred in bridge construction and sea wall improvement were to prove a millstone around the tramway's neck for many years to come.

The introduction of trams did much to stimulate growth in hitherto undeveloped areas of the town.

### Additions to the Pier

As for waterborne transport, improvements to the pierhead were needed to accommodate larger ships and to circumvent the problems of silting up channels. In 1898 the pier was extended another 150 yards into deeper water, reaching its current 1.33 miles, and in the same year the landward end was made more attractive by the provision of a complex of 'Pier Hill Buildings' which included a bandstand, seawater baths, restaurants, shops and shelters. These were demolished in the 1970s, but there is still evidence below Pier Hill of where they stood.

From *c*.1901-4 a new attraction – a waterchute – was operated on the east side of the pier, but this did not prove a success. The waterchute basin was later used as a swimming pool and a boating lake and in more recent times it was home to a replica of the *Golden Hind*. 'Blackbeard's Pirate Adventure', part of the 1990s 'Adventure Island' development, now occupies the spot.

In 1908 yet more improvements were made to the pierhead, with the addition of an Upper Promenade Deck and a bandstand. Concerts on the pier were provided for many years by Adam Seebold and his orchestra.

### Entertainment and Leisure

Bandstands also existed on Pier Hill, Marine Parade, 'Happy Valley' (the cliffs to the west of the pier) and on the cliffs in Clifftown Parade (where a later bandstand survives to this day). The Marine Parade bandstand once played host to song-and-dance and comedy acts such as the Jolly Boys. Chirgwin's Concert Party was another famous attraction.

**75** The Pier Hill Buildings, which stood below Pier Hill, pictured *c.*1898. This entertainment complex of restaurants and amusements was demolished in the 1970s. Close examination of the hill here, however, reveals steps and associated brickwork that were once part of the complex.

**76** The pierhead extension and promenade under construction in 1908.

**77** The *Plough* and *Palace Theatre* on the London Road at its junction with West Road in Westcliff in 1922 during the making up of the road. Although traffic was growing in Southend at this time, the absence of vehicles, compared with this junction today, is noticeably marked!

Thomas Trotter's old seafront theatre had long since disappeared, but was superseded by the time of the Town Council by the *Alexandra Theatre*, built on the site of the Public Hall in Alexandra Street, itself barely 20 years old. The theatre was destroyed by fire in 1895 but in the following year rose from the flames as the new *Empire Theatre*. There were other theatres in Tylers Avenue, Grove Terrace and elsewhere. Perhaps the most notable from a modern perspective is the *Palace Theatre* in London Road, Westcliff, erected in 1912, which remains one of the town's principal theatres.

At this period the first moving pictures to be shown in Southend — footage of the Boer War — were displayed at the since-disappeared Criterion Palace of Varieties on Marine Parade. Films were also shown in the Pier Pavilion and at various converted theatres in the town. By 1910 the first purpose-built cinemas were also making an appearance, though this new form of entertainment did not become very popular until after the First World War.

Southend also gained its first professional football team during this period; in 1906 Southend United were founded. Their HQ was the *Blue Boar* in Prittlewell and their ground was just across West Street at a place called Roots Hall. This name was a corruption of 'Roward's Hall', a once-impressive but long-vanished residence in whose grounds the team's pitch was laid out. The club began life in the Southern League, playing at Roots Hall until the First World War, when the lease ran out and the ground was converted into allotments for the

**78** A plaque on the *Blue Boar* commemorating the founding of Southend United Football Club in the building in 1906.

war effort. It would be some forty years and two different grounds before the club returned there.

Other attractions included a skating rink at the *Alexandra Theatre* complex and a 'switchback' rollercoaster ride at Southend's first major fairground, erected *c*.1889 on top of Pier Hill (though this only lasted a few years).

**79**   Southend pier, *c.*1893, showing (in the background, top right) the town's first fairground, on the site now occupied by the *Palace Hotel.*

**80**   The Warwick Tower, *c.*1905 — one of the main early rides at the Kursaal.

In 1895 Dowsett, Ingram and Baxter gave land for a new park to the east of Old Southend on the marshy low-lying areas of Southchurch parish. This later became Southchurch Park and a home to county cricket (played there to this day). The Park covers part of the old Bronze Age lagoon and the lakes there are a survival of this.

In 1894 Bernard Wilshire Tolhurst donated a sizeable piece of land to the north-east of the *Minerva* for what was then called Marine Park. Originally featuring a cricket pitch and football ground, plus a trotting track and cycling facilities, the park evolved over the next decade into an amusement centre whose name would become synonymous with Southend — the Kursaal.

### The Kursaal

The Kursaal took its name from the company behind it — Southend & Margate Kursaals Ltd. It opened

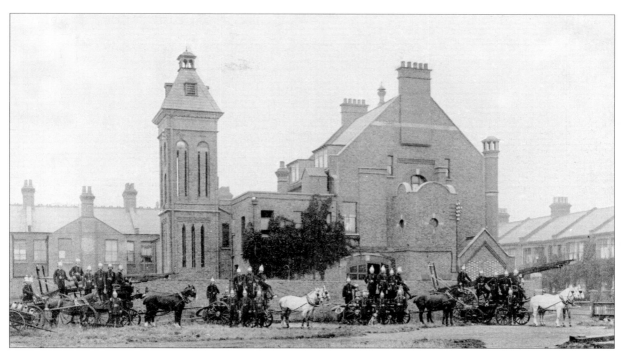

**81**   The town's first purpose-built fire station in Tylers Avenue, 1906.

in 1901. Its famous dome became a symbol of local entertainment.

The whole complex was packed with rides and amusements and it grew over the next 50 years to become one of Southend's principal tourist attractions and the largest park of its kind in the south of England. The Aerial Flight, and later the waterchute and Togo the snake charmer, were amongst its many attractions and the park even received a visit from Barnum & Bailey's famous circus. One of the most distinctive early rides was the revolving 'Warwick Tower', which stood next to the *Britannia* pub and ran from 1898 to 1905.

## Public Services
In 1893 Southend's hitherto voluntary fire brigade was taken over by the Town Council and established under the captaincy of Harry Garon on a more permanent basis, now being financed from the rates rather than by voluntary contributions. In 1902 for the first time the brigade was provided with purpose-built, centrally-placed headquarters with a new station opening in Tylers Avenue. As

the town expanded, a sub-station was also set up at the *Cricketers* to serve Westcliff.

In 1898, aware of the growing population and the need to house those who could not afford to house themselves, the Council moved towards setting up a Housing of the Working Classes Committee and began to look for somewhere to build. In 1900 it settled on a site on the east side of Sutton Road on the Priory Farm Estate and within the next few years 40 such houses were erected in a new road – Ruskin Avenue.

In health, the Southend Victoria Hospital was complemented by a new 'infectious diseases' hospital (also known as the Borough Sanatorium) in Balmoral Road, Westcliff. This became known as Westcliff Hospital and survived until the 1990s, when the site was developed for housing.

By the mid-1890s the need for another burial ground was already being discussed. The Parish Burial Ground in North Road, a replacement for the churchyard at St Mary's and opened in only 1881, was already beginning to fill. It was anticipated that there was only six years' capacity left. The

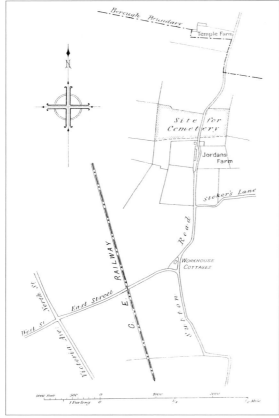

**82** Sutton Road in 1914, looking north towards Ruskin Avenue (on the right), where the town's first Council houses were built.

**83** A map showing the proposed site for the (Sutton Road) cemetery, which opened in the late 1890s. Stoker's Lane (right) was later incorporated into what is now Eastern Avenue.

situation at St John's was even more acute – the churchyard was virtually up to maximum. With the prospect of Southchurch being taken over and the Borough clearly heading for more expansion, a new cemetery was essential.

In 1895 a site in Sutton Road was identified in an area then known as Jordan's Farm and by 1900 this had opened and began to accept admissions. Once St John's churchyard and the Parish Burial Ground were full, all burials would henceforth take place there.

**Education and Learning**

In 1893 the Council set up a Technical Instruction Committee to oversee education in the town. This included representatives from the Southend Institute, Essex County Council and the Southend-on-Sea School Board, which had replaced the Prittlewell School Board on incorporation the previous year.

**84** The Technical School (top left), *c*.1910, showing the tramlines leading from the High Street to Prittlewell via Victoria Avenue.

In 1895 a new 'Technical School' was erected next to the Institute in Clarence Road and the whole complex, shared between the School and the Council, became known as the 'Municipal Buildings'. Within a year, however, the school was outgrowing its premises and in 1902 it moved to a brand new, purpose-built Technical School at Victoria Circus. The building, designed by H.T. Hare, stood on the north-west corner of the crossroads/roundabout and soon became one of the main focal points at the top end of the High Street. *The Buildings of England* author, Sir Nikolaus Pevsner, thought it 'quite decorative and successful as a showpiece'. It was demolished in 1971, though the brick boundary pillars and grass approaches remained until the mid-1990s.

1902 saw a new Education Act and in 1903 the Technical Instruction Committee and Southend-on-Sea School Board were replaced by a new Education Committee. The Council took the opportunity for a full review of the existing education provision in the town. It found that there were eight other schools in operation (all for infants and juniors) – Prittlewell Church School in East Street, Southend's National School in Eastern Esplanade, Southchurch National School, London Road School, Brewery Road School (now Porters Grange), Leigh Road School (later called Hamlet Court School and now demolished), St Helen's Roman Catholic School and an as yet incomplete school, Southchurch Hall, in Ambleside Drive (completed in 1904).

This was considered insufficient and in 1904 the Council bought land on the corner of London and Leigh Roads near Chalkwell Park for a new

**85**   Bournemouth Park Road in 1908, showing (background, centre) Bournemouth Park School. Side streets are appearing, but beyond the school are open fields.

Chalkwell Hall School (opened in 1909) and a site in Bournemouth Park Road for what was to become Bournemouth Park School (opened in 1907). In 1905 it also bought a site in MacDonald Avenue for what became Westborough School (opened in 1912).

The Council even advanced the cause of female representation by insisting in 1910 that, of the 19 members of the Education Committee (10 councillors, nine others), one of the 'others' had to be a woman.

By 1912 the Technical School had reached its capacity and the following year the girls were moved out to a new building in Boston Avenue (now St Mary's Prittlewell – Church of England (Aided) Primary School). This new school became Southend High School for Girls and the Technical School, no longer mixed, was renamed Southend High School for Boys.

In 1903 the millionaire philanthropist, Andrew Carnegie, offered £8,000 towards the construction of a public library if the Council would adopt the provisions of libraries legislation and find a site for the building. There had been libraries in Southend before, but this would be the first to be open to all.

By 1904 the Council had set up a Public Libraries Committee, found a site in Victoria Avenue and commissioned the Technical College architect H.T. Hare to design a building. The library opened in July 1906 and by November it had attracted 5,000 members! It survives as the Central Museum, with a new (1974) library built next door.

**The Church**

Several new churches were also built during this period: St Alban's (1898), St Mark's (1901), St Erkenwald's (1905) and St Saviour's (1911) and a mission church at Southchurch Beach. Southend's original church, St John the Baptist, was enlarged. St Erkenwald's, an imposing yellow brick building which stood at the north-east corner of York

**86** The new Public Library (now the Central Museum) in Victoria Avenue, pictured in 1912. The railings and shrubs have now gone to accommodate the modern dual carriageway.

**87** Demolition of the Grade II*-listed 1905 St Erkenwald's Church in York Road in 1995, which went ahead despite a campaign by conservationists to preserve it.

**88**   One of the Garon family's many shops in Southend High Street, 1912.

Road and Southchurch Avenue, on land purchased with the aid of William Gregson, was a distinctive landmark in the east of the town. Designed by Walter Tapper, it was demolished amid public outcry in April 1995, despite carrying a Grade II* listing.

There were churches of other denominations, including Chelmsford Avenue (1901), on land given by Thomas Dowsett and the Reverend Arthur Sadd, and Crowstone Congregational Church (1910) in Crowstone Road, Westcliff.

### Business

In commerce, the High Street was confirmed in the 1890s as the focal point of shopping in the town and several well-known businesses were established there. Brightwell, Dowsett and the Garon family all had shops in the town centre, as did another one-time councillor, Robert Arthur ('R.A.') Jones, who built up a profitable jewellery business.

Schofield & Martin's, Raven's, Keddie's, Cotgrove's and many others all became household names. The Garon family in particular saw much success, diversifying and expanding until by the late 1940s they owned 37 shops, plus a bakery, a hotel and even a cinema!

Several new hotels were built during this period, perhaps the most conspicuous being the *Hotel Metropole*, erected shortly after the turn of the century on land immediately to the south of St John's on the site of the old funfair. This distinctive new building, which still dominates the skyline, was later renamed the *Palace Hotel*.

The *Hotel Victoria* opened at Victoria Circus in 1899. Like the Technical College diagonally opposite, it quickly became a focal point of the town.

The *Queens Hotel* in Hamlet Court Road and the *Westcliff*, *Overcliff* and *Westward Ho Hotels* all opened during this period. All except the *Westcliff* have now gone.

**89** Pier Hill, *c.*1892, showing (top left) a board announcing the impending construction of the *Hotel Metropole* (later the *Palace Hotel*).

In 1906 a suggestion to change the name of the town to 'Thamesmouth', presumably for business reasons, never made any progress.

## Literature

Southend was host to several men of literature during the years of the Town Council. They included the poet, Robert Buchanan, who is buried at St John's, and Southend's most famous literary son, novelist Warwick Deeping, who was born in the town in 1877. His father, Dr. George Deeping, and grandfather, Dr. Warwick, were both active in local affairs. There is a monument to Deeping at St John's, not far from that to Buchanan.

Perhaps the most important book of the period, however, is Southend's first history book, the 1909 *Southend-on-Sea & District* by John William Burrows, son of John H. Burrows and his successor as editor of the *Southend Standard*. The only previous book to give the history of the post-1856 town

was Philip Benton's *The History of Rochford Hundred* (published 1867-88), but this dealt with the Hundred's history in parishes and Southend therefore was a small section hidden in the Prittlewell chapter. Burrows' intention was to correct the mistaken view that Southend had nothing of historical interest, but he also reported on Southend in his day and the book gives a valuable insight into the early days of the Town Council as well of the older history of the area.

## Thorpe Bay

By the time of Burrows' book, Southend had expanded westwards as far as it could go – to the boundary with Leigh-on-Sea. Since the acquisition of Southchurch, expansion had also been taking place eastwards and in 1909 Burrows made passing reference to a scheme to convert 'Thorpe Hall Bay' in that parish into a 'high-class residential resort'.

**90**    Thorpe Esplanade in 1911. The fledgling resort of Thorpe Bay is beginning to take shape in the background.

The Thorpe Hall estate had by this time been bought by Colonel Ynyr Henry Burges. In 1907 Thorpe Hall itself had been converted into a golf club and by 1910 streets to the east of Thorpe Hall Avenue were being laid out. Burges had earlier disagreed with the Council over their proposals for trams across his land, but there is no doubt that the construction of the leafy Boulevards in 1913-4 helped to enhance the appeal of his estate. Burges hailed from Northern Ireland and several of the early street names – Tyrone Road, Parkanaur Avenue and others – were taken from his native country. The golf club was deliberately established to attract potential residents.

At Westcliff, the opening of the railway station had helped to boost residential development and it was agreed that a station for this new resort could have the same effect. The station was originally to be called 'Southchurch-on-Sea', and it did open under that name in July 1910, but after a few days influential residents had it changed to 'Thorpe Bay' – the 'bay' being added to the old 'Thorpe' manor name to give a new, prestigious name for a new, prestigious resort. Development was substantially delayed however by the advent of the First World War.

**Greater Representation and Further Expansion**
In 1910 the number of electoral wards in the town was increased from three to eight – Chalkwell, Milton, Pier, Prittlewell, Southchurch, Thorpe, Victoria and Westborough. The number of aldermen was also increased. There were now 24 councillors (instead of 18) and eight aldermen (instead of six). The November 1910 elections saw the arrival of the Council's first female councillor – Miss Elizabeth Bannester.

**91** Leigh Road in 1912, with Chalkwell Park on the left. Leigh Road originally went left of the house in the distance, but a more direct route was built to the right of the house as the bends and gradients in the old road were too difficult for trams to negotiate. The left hand road is known to this day as Old Leigh Road.

The Council was also thinking about applying for the town's administrative promotion to 'County Borough' status, which would give it control over various aspects of administration currently handled by the County Council. Amongst the most significant would be highways/transport matters and the creation of a Southend police force. Since 1906 there had also been talk of seeking further enlargement of the Borough by incorporating Leigh,

and in 1912 it was decided to combine the two applications and seek elevation and expansion under one Parliamentary Bill.

The next parish beyond Leigh to the west – Hadleigh – had expressed interest in being included in any expansion, but the Council was against this. However, part of Eastwood, the parish to the north of Southend Borough which also abutted onto Leigh, was to be included.

**92**   Leigh church, *c.*1893. The centre of Leigh moved during the late 19th and early 20th centuries from the maritime village below the church to the area to the right of and behind the photographer (the Broadway). The house in the distance was demolished in the 1920s to accommodate a new road (Broadway West).

The Southend-on-Sea Corporation Act 1913 confirmed all these proposals. Leigh and part of Eastwood were included in the Borough from 9 November 1913 and the newly enlarged administrative area was promoted to County Borough status with effect from 1 April 1914.

**Leigh**

Leigh already had a direct connection with Southend – through the tramway network – and it was perhaps to be expected that it would be next on the list for the expanding town. Nevertheless, Leigh was a different prospect from Southchurch, a lot larger and more developed, with its own Urban District Council and a distinct community identity.

Historically, Leigh was a maritime community, with houses, pubs and shops huddled together in the High Street and the 15th-century church of St Clement dominating the skyline on the hill above. Like long-lost Milton it had proud traditions as a

port and shipbuilding centre, at its peak in the 16th and 17th centuries. The *Mayflower* was said to have stopped there on its history-making voyage to the New World in 1620 and Leigh men and ships had served in wars against the French, Dutch and Spanish. Several Leigh sons had grown up to be captains or admirals in the Navy and many, such as the Haddocks, the Salmons, the Goodlads and the Chesters, are commemorated by brasses and monuments in the church.

The village had close associations with Trinity House, as well as a Coastguard Station and a Custom House. Smuggling had been rife in Leigh over the years and as recently as 1892 a fire at the *Peter Boat* public house – attended by Southend Fire Brigade – had revealed a hidden underground storage room, accessible from the river.

At the time of Domesday Book Leigh was in the ownership of Ranulf Peverel. It later passed through the Rich/Warwick line (sometime owners of land in both Prittlewell and Southchurch) to its best known benefactor, Lady Olivia Sparrow, who sank wells and founded a school in the mid-19th century. The village had strong Methodist connections — John Wesley visited half a dozen times between 1748 and 1756. The painter, John Constable, is also said to have visited.

For centuries Leigh remained a small waterside village, with a few houses straggling up the hill towards the church. The rest of the parish was dotted with farms, notably the manor house, Leigh Hall, which stood to the north-east of the church at what is now the junction of Leigh Hall Road and Pall Mall.

The arrival of the railway in the mid-1850s, however, led to its complete transformation. Due to local geography — a low shoreline, hemmed in by steep hills — it was decided to lay the railway line right through the centre of the old fishing village, immediately to the north of the High Street, and many of the village's old buildings were destroyed.

Forty years later a future Southend mayor, Frederick Francis Ramuz, bought up over 300 acres of land on the hill above the old fishing village and began to sell it off for development. This included Leigh Hall Farm and Victoria Pottery, which was situated on the boundary between Leigh and Prittlewell. As more and more houses were built the focus of the Leigh community began to shift from the High Street to a new shopping street, The Broadway (formerly Hall Road), and the old fishing village — the 'Old Town' or 'Old Leigh' as it became — gradually got left behind.

Leigh church — on the site of an earlier building — had been largely untouched since the 15th century, save for the addition of a red-brick Tudor porch. However, as the town expanded around it, it quickly underwent three extensions, being provided with a new chancel, south aisle and lady chapel/north east vestries between 1872 and 1913.

By 1913, when Leigh was absorbed into Southend, it was an established, self-contained, growing town. It had its own gas and sewage works, its own fire brigade and police officers, its own Council Offices, its own schools and its own burial ground (on the London Road — still there). The roads were made up, water was supplied and of course it had the trams.

It also had a strong community spirit, built in the fishing village where generations of Leigh families had lived and died, and, although the transition was relatively smooth, the town retains a distinct community feel to this day.

**County Borough Status**

There were many challenges ahead for the expanded County Borough. It now comprised three historic communities — Prittlewell, Southchurch and Leigh — and four modern ones — Southend itself, Westcliff, Chalkwell and Thorpe Bay — plus a bit of Eastwood! There were inconsistencies in the infrastructure and the rates and yet more increased representation was required, with two new wards (Leigh and St Clement's) representing Leigh, each with three councillors.

The population had jumped by another 10,000 with Leigh's acquisition, taking the total to a massive 80,000 (compared with 27,000 in 1901!). There was a new police force to set up and run, a new coat of arms (featuring emblems from Prittlewell, Southchurch, Leigh and Eastwood) and a new Borough motto, *Per Mare Per Ecclesiam* (By the Sea, By the Church).

Things looked good for Southend in April 1914, but an unexpected development lay just around the corner — war!

# *Six*

# From One War to the Next

**The First World War**

Southend had an early taste of what war might mean, having a peacetime visit in July 1909 from the British Home and Atlantic Fleets and accompanying Cruiser Squadron. One hundred and forty-nine ships anchored in the Thames for over a week and thousands of sailors enjoyed shore leave in the resort. The exercise was designed to give publicity to the Admiralty, who hoped it would generate public support for further warship building, and it was the first of several major peacetime naval visits to the town over the next 40 years.

At the start of the war Germany's Zeppelin airships were predicted to be one of the most potent weapons on either side and Southend, as a coastal town, was vulnerable. In May 1915 there were two major attacks.

**93** The Essex Regiment in Southend in 1915, showing a poster advertising warnings of air-raids.

The first, on 10 May, destroyed the Cromwell Boarding Establishment in London Road and damaged houses in West Road (Prittlewell) and Baxter Avenue. One person was killed – a prominent Salvation Army member, Mrs. Whitwell. Parts of Leigh and Westcliff were also attacked and there was a near-miss at the Boys' School when a bomb embedded itself in the roadway at Victoria Circus. An anti-English message was dropped from one of the Zeppelins, stating that the attackers would 'kill or cure' the population.

People were incensed by the effrontery of the attack and organised a riot against German shops. A local newspaper, the *Southend & Westcliff Graphic*, was equally aggressive in its editorial, commenting that 'the person with German blood in him is rightly considered to be a dangerous enemy'.

The second raid, a fortnight later, claimed two more victims – a seven-year-old girl living in Broadway Market (a street off Victoria Avenue near Victoria Circus) and an unfortunate female visitor to Southbourne Grove in Westcliff who was killed by falling shrapnel from an anti-aircraft gun. Leigh and Southchurch were also badly hit.

By 1916 Britain's air defences were beginning to cope with Zeppelin attacks and in March Zeppelin L15 was shot down over Southend and crashed into the Thames. The following year, however, a new threat – Gotha bombers (aeroplanes) – appeared in the skies and on 12 August 1917 the worst attack of the war resulted in massive damage to central Southend and the deaths of more than 30 people.

The town was in the forefront of home-based activity throughout the war; prison ships for British-based German civilians took their charges on board at the end of the pier and the *Palace Hotel* was converted for use as 'Queen Mary's Naval Hospital',

**94**   A house in London Road, Southend, damaged by Zeppelin bombing in May 1915.

**95**   Southend's mayor, Joseph Francis, and Chief Constable, H. M. Kerslake, with the town's new police force in 1914.

where it received both British and Belgian patients. Soldiers were billeted in the town, the National Guard drilled in local parks and communal kitchens were set up. In 1916 the Council noted a 'decrease of population of the Borough caused largely by the patriotic response of its eligible male population to the call of His Majesty for recruits'. The King and Queen, and the Lord Mayor of London, all visited the area during the war.

The end of the war in November 1918 was signalled by the siren at Southend gasworks. The Mayor, Joseph Francis, who had held the post throughout the war, became the first person to be given the Freedom of the Borough for his services to Southend.

On 19 July 1919, officially designated 'Peace Day', the Naval Fleet visited again and there were decorations, bonfires and fireworks in the town.

In 1920 Victory Path in Chalkwell was established and in 1921 a war memorial, designed by the London Cenotaph designer Sir Edwin Lutyens, was unveiled on the cliffs.

**Continuing Development**

After the war, development restarted – and with Leigh now in the borough there was even more land available for the town, with gradual progress from the old borough boundary to the new one. Existing Leigh streets were made up and new estates laid out. By the 1920s the Marine and Highland Estates in westernmost Leigh were being developed. Eastwood Road, connecting the London Road at West Leigh to Eastwood, was made up and widened and land at Belfairs was beginning to be developed.

To the north of central Southend, in Prittlewell, development began to extend across Prittle Brook at

**96** Eastwood Road, 1913, looking north from the brook. The line of the road looks familiar but there are no houses on either side. It was the making up of this road which helped the development of the Belfairs area as Southend expanded into what had been the old Leigh parish.

**97** Southbourne Grove in 1914, showing bridge widening. Bridges were built over the brook from the First World War onwards and streets made up beyond them as Southend extended northwards to fill undeveloped areas of the former Prittlewell parish.

**98**   The Southend Arterial Road (the A127) near Dulverton Avenue in 1921, during its construction. The two houses are still there, though the course of the road at this point has changed.

Fairfax Drive and up onto the lands of the Earls Hall Estate. New bridges were built over the brook (gradually being straightened in man-made channels) at Gainsborough Drive, Springfield Drive and Highfield Crescent, and Southbourne and Westbourne Groves were gradually extended northwards. Streets around Carlton Avenue and Carlingford Drive were also laid out.

In Southchurch there was further development around Hamstel Road and, in the east, Thorpe Bay continued to grow as development progressed slowly but surely eastwards towards Shoebury. This had reached such an extent by the 1920s that two new ecclesiastical parishes – St Augustine's and Christchurch – had to be formed out of the old Southchurch parish.

By 1921 the population of the town had grown to around 106,000 – four times that of 20 years earlier!

Aware of the increasing need for local authority housing, the Council expanded its Sutton Road (Ruskin Avenue) development and provided new council housing areas in Leigh (Middlesex Avenue area and a small development in East Street) and in Fairfax Drive. Unemployment, a big problem in the inter-war period, was ameliorated by using local labour to make up, widen and generally improve the town's roads.

The road network was in fact dramatically improved during the 1920s by the introduction of several major new thoroughfares. The most important was a brand new road from London – the Southend Arterial Road (now the A127) – which was part-funded by the government and formally opened on 25 March 1925 by H.R.H. Prince Henry, after whom the last section, 'Prince Avenue', is named. The mid-1920s also saw the

**99**   This, unbelievably, is Priory Crescent on the east side of Priory Park (the trees on the left), pictured during construction in 1923. The tall chimney in the background marks the sewage works (which is still there) and the bridge on the right carries the road over the railway from Priory Crescent to Eastern Avenue. The area on the right is now occupied by housing.

**100**   Eastern Avenue during construction in 1926. The field on the right behind the fence is now the Jones Memorial Ground.

**101**   Cuckoo Corner in 1923, showing the construction of Priory Crescent and, in the distance, the chimney at the sewage works. Until this time Cuckoo Corner was just that – a corner or bend in the road. The construction of Priory Crescent and, in the late 1930s, Manners Way (out of the picture to the left) would transform it into a (busy) roundabout. Priory Park is on the right; the land on the left is now occupied by housing.

**102**   Believe it or not, this is Prittlewell Chase, pictured in 1922 with Cardigan Avenue going off to the right in the background. The whole Prittlewell Chase/Kenilworth Gardens/Blenheim Chase route was constructed over a period from the 1920s to the 1950s.

**103**  Eastwood Boulevard, then called Eastwood Lane, in 1915. This ancient track led from Chalkwell Hall to Eastwood in a roughly north-westerly direction and this section of it was intended to be converted into a dual-carriageway boulevard. In the event, however, only the eastern carriageway was built. The fields to the top left would later be occupied by Westcliff High School.

construction of Priory Crescent – a new road around the north and east sides of Priory Park which linked via a bridge over the railway to another new road, Eastern Avenue, which followed in part the line of an existing road. (Priory Crescent on the south side also replaced an existing street – Brook Road.) Eastern Avenue led initially to Sutton Road and then to Hamstel Road – the link to Bournes Green came much later. This whole route, effectively a bypass for Central Southend, provided much more direct access to the east side of the town. With the construction of Lifstan Way to the south of Hamstel Road in the 1930s it also provided direct access to the seafront. These changes created a new road junction – Cuckoo Corner roundabout – which was to become one of the main traffic focal points in the town.

Traffic was steadily growing throughout Southend and several measures were taken to deal with it. The success of the Boulevard schemes in Southchurch and Thorpe Bay led to similar schemes being tried elsewhere. The Prittlewell Chase/Kenilworth Gardens/Blenheim Chase route was constructed during the 1920s and 1930s, with a planned dual-carriageway Eastwood Boulevard feeder (though only the eastern half of the latter was built). (Eastwood Boulevard, nowhere near Eastwood, follows the line of an old road called Eastwood Lane, which led from Chalkwell Hall to Eastwood in a roughly north-westerly direction.) Later, as the Borough's streets extended through Leigh towards the Hadleigh boundary, Highlands and Sutherland Boulevards were laid out.

In the old Prittlewell village a road-widening and clearance scheme for Victoria Avenue ripped

**104**   Victoria Avenue, looking north towards the library, in 1923.

the heart out of the historic community and demolished many of its oldest and most valuable buildings. This 'Prittlewell Improvement Scheme', as it was called, started in 1912 with the demolition of houses in front of the church to open up a better view of the building. It was superseded in 1918 by the Prittlewell War Memorial Scheme which continued building demolition and road-widening and introduced improvements to Prittlewell churchyard (with a new lychgate and memorial cross to those killed in the First World War). This process of 'improvement' continued into the 1930s and led to the loss of many of Southend's oldest and finest secular buildings.

Traffic problems were a growing concern in the early 1920s. Even in 1915 the Council had imposed a 10mph speed limit in some streets and there were constant complaints over the next decade about speeding motor vehicles in the town. By 1924 policemen were on point duty at busy junctions, including Victoria Circus and at London Road/Hamlet Court Road 'in view of the great volume of traffic' there. In 1932 'automatic traffic control signals' were ordered for the latter junction and also for High Street/Alexandra Street and the *Blue Boar*. Car-parking was also becoming an issue and in 1929 Councillor Mrs. Constance Leyland proposed that a Special Committee should be set up 'to consider the question of providing adequate and convenient parking places for cars, sufficient not only for present requirements, but for the yearly increase in numbers which will undoubtedly take place for a considerable time to come'. The seafront was a particular problem and in the early 1930s the gardens in the middle of Western Esplanade were removed for the area to be laid out for parking. Parking provision had already been made by this stage on Eastern Esplanade, when the old *Castle Hotel* and neighbouring Castle Terrace were demolished in the 1920s.

As Southend expanded, the essential services – gas, water, electricity – were connected to outlying parts of the Borough. The gasworks, acquired by the Borough Council in 1913, was transferred to the Southend Gas Company in 1922 (the latter being taken over by the Gas, Light and Coke Company 10 years later).

Several new schools were built, many being sited on what were then the fringes of the town. These included Fairfax and Westcliff High (the latter of which began life in Victoria Avenue as the Commercial School) (both 1920s) and Wentworth (now Cecil Jones Lower School), Thorpe, Earls Hall and a new Southend High School for Boys in Prittlewell Chase (all 1930s). The old Southend High School for Boys at Victoria Circus reverted to Technical College status. Another old school – the National School on Eastern Esplanade – was demolished in 1925.

## Age of Benevolence

With development continuing, the importance of retaining public open spaces and protecting the town's heritage was not lost on several influential people.

Arguably the most important of them was the wealthy High Street jeweller and one-time councillor, R.A. Jones. Over a period of eight years from 1913-21 Jones gave three substantial tracts of land – the Jones Memorial Ground, Priory Park and the Victory Sports Ground – to the town for public use to complement other smaller gifts that he had been providing since the 1890s (clocks, public seats, sports trophies, etc.).

The Jones Memorial Ground (1913), in memory of his wife, was given as playing fields for the town's elementary school children.

**105**   Robert Arthur (R.A.) Jones, one of the town's greatest benefactors.

Prittlewell Priory and the surrounding 30 acres of parkland (1917) were given to the town for a museum and public park. Due to the war, the park was not formally opened until 1920, when the official opening ceremony was carried out by the Duke of York (later King George VI). The Priory was restored and opened as a museum two years later. The opening ceremony was performed by Sir C. Hercules Reid (President of the Society of Antiquaries), in the company of the Mayor (Sir John Francis) and numerous other dignitaries.

The Victory Sports Ground (1921) was given in memory of sportsmen from the Borough who had fought and died in the First World War.

In recognition of his outstanding generosity, Jones was made a Freeman of the Borough and given the MBE. When he died in 1925, he was buried beneath a cross in the cloister garth of the Priory which he had donated. His son, Edward Cecil Jones, who also served as a councillor and gave much of his own personal fortune to the town, was buried beside him when he died in 1967.

**106**   Part of the celebrations for the opening of Priory Park in 1920, with the unveiling of the drinking fountain by the Duke of York.

**107**   Sutton Road in 1921, looking towards the entrance gate for the Victory Sports Ground. The building on the left is the old workhouse.

**108**   Southchurch Hall during restoration work in 1929.

In 1925 the family of Thomas Dowsett (Southend's first mayor) proved equally benevolent, with the gift of the 13th-century Southchurch Hall and surrounding parkland to the town. The Hall was restored before being formally opened to the public in 1931 by the Dowsett family and that year's mayor, Alderman Albert Martin. It became Southchurch library, serving in that capacity until 1974. Southchurch Park, which had hitherto been known as Southchurch Hall Park, was renamed to avoid any confusion.

A third ancient building also became public property around this time with the acquisition by the Council in 1932 of Porters from Sir Charles Nicholson. This, too, underwent extensive restoration and opened in 1935 as the mayor's parlour and civic house.

The interest in Southend's history, inspired by the opening of Prittlewell Priory and the creation of a museum there, led to the formation in 1920 of the Southend & District Antiquarian & Historical Society by three local notables – John William Burrows (the newspaper editor and local historian), William Pollitt (the borough librarian) and Herbert Tompkins (a local author). The Society went on to publish many articles about Southend's history.

**Public Transport**

The First World War had caused a lull in the development of Southend's tramway network and the whole service was reduced for much of the war. Three wagons were introduced to ferry coal from an improved Corporation loading jetty in Eastern Esplanade to the electricity generating station at the depot in London Road. Soldiers outnumbered

**109**   The first tram to go round Warrior Square, 1921.

civilians on many journeys, particularly in the east where troops from Shoebury garrison were frequent users of the Boulevard service.

After the war some changes were made to tramway routes, including the introduction of a new loop round Warrior Square to alleviate traffic problems in the High Street. By the mid-1920s the trams were at their height, but other forms of transport were now competing for custom.

From 1925 onwards the Council began to use trolley buses (also powered by electricity from overhead wires but running on rubber tyres rather than rails) and these began gradually to replace tram services. The introduction of trolley buses enabled several new public transport routes, reaching, for example, Eastwood Boulevard in the west and Hamstel Road in the east.

The real boon to travellers at this period, however, was the petrol-engined motor bus which was increasingly coming into use. They could be driven anywhere in the town without the need for rails or overhead wires. The Council had experimented with motor buses before, but it was not until the early 1930s that it decided to embrace them completely. By this stage, however, several private companies were operating and competition was fierce.

**110**   A trolley bus in Quebec Avenue, 1930.

Ritchie Bridge) and was responsible for developing some of the land there near Eastwood Rise and Tudor Road, where some of the grounds of Edwards Hall survive as Edwards Hall Park. Building was actually the family's principal business, but their Eastwood estate was badly situated (no railway stations and poor bus services), and so they decided to set up their own company.

For many years W.M.S. and Southend Council had an agreement whereby the Council could only operate buses in the eastern half of the town and W.M.S. only in the west.

Another large bus company serving Southend at this period was Eastern National, which went on to become one of the largest of all.

By the 1930s, with the success of trolley and motor buses, the days of the Southend trams were numbered. In 1932 the tramway office at Victoria Circus was demolished for road improvements and, as older trams fell out of service, they were not replaced. The novelty of travelling on them simply for pleasure had long since worn off, nationwide industrial depression was biting, tracks needed repair and operating costs were mounting, so it was decided to phase them out. The last tram ran on 8 April 1942.

### Railways

The inter-war period saw several substantial changes to the Borough's railway service; two new stations were built and a third was relocated.

The first new station was at Southend East (1931), serving Southchurch, but deliberately named so as

One of the best-known local bus companies was Westcliff-on-Sea Motor Services Ltd (W.M.S. for short) which began life in 1914 as the Westcliff-on-Sea Charabanc Company. The company had expanded successfully throughout the late 1910s and '20s until in 1927 it took over another well-known local company, Edwards Hall Motors (E.H.M.), owned by the Leigh- and Eastwood-based Bridge family. By the mid-1930s, when under the control of the Tilling group, it even offered (unsuccessfully) to take over the Borough Council's bus operation!

The Bridge family had taken its company's name from Edwards Hall in Eastwood (owned by Henry

**111**    The bridge over the railway at Chalkwell station in 1911 — 20 years before the station was built!

to attract excursion traffic away from central Southend and spread it out across the town. The second was at Chalkwell (1933), built in an attractive seafront location to serve the rapidly expanded suburb there.

The relocated station was at Leigh, whose original station and neighbouring level-crossing (now gone) in the Old Town High Street had been attracting criticism (because of danger and congestion) since as early as 1913. This, and the difficulties of accommodating goods traffic, led to a move half a mile to the west (its current location) where it became operational on 1 January 1934.

In 1923 there was a nationwide reorganisation into four big railway companies and Southend found itself served by the L.N.E.R. and L.M.S. (at the Victoria and Central stations respectively). This was

a period of heavy railway usage and the late 1920s and early 1930s saw huge crowds of train travellers arriving in the town.

### Entertainment
Trains, buses and charabancs brought thousands of visitors to the town in search of entertainment and Southend had plenty to offer.

The author, V. E. Burrows, remembering 1925, spoke of horse-drawn mystery tours, charabanc and coach tours, amusements, cafés, Southend Rock, shellfish and boarding houses and bed & breakfast places in all the side streets off the seafront. The stretch from the Kursaal to Thorpe Bay (now boasting, amongst other things, a miniature golf course) was as bustling and busy as Marine Parade. Men preached on the beach and there was an occasional battleship seen in the river.

**112** Construction work on the new Westcliff Swimming Baths (now the Westcliff Leisure Centre) in 1914.

The Council-owned Westcliff Swimming Baths (now the privately-owned Westcliff Leisure Centre) opened on Western Esplanade in 1915, replacing some floating baths, run by the Absalom family in the period before the First World War. Though open-air, they proved popular with residents and visitors alike, as did Annual Yachting Week – visited twice in the early 1920s by King George V.

The Kursaal – 'the matchless Cockney paradise' – was as popular as ever with its rides and side-shows and when the Illuminations (fairy lights on the esplanades, cliffs and pier) were introduced in the mid-1930s the town was second only to Black-pool in popularity. The cliffs also featured a new attraction – 'Never Never Land' – a series of illu-minated characters from children's stories, set in the Shrubbery below Royal Terrace. Visitors, as

ever principally from London, poured into the town, which became a popular destination for coach trips whilst retaining a regular steamer service on the river.

The pier, which had by now been welcoming visitors for a century, was further extended to en-able it to handle more and larger ships and in 1929 this extension was opened by H.R.H. Prince George. Pleasure trips were now available not only to and from London, but also to Margate and even the Continent. The seaward end of the pier was home to Louis Tussaud's waxworks. The pier's railway track was doubled to cope with the in-creasing traffic.

The 1885 tollhouse at the landward end of the pier could not cope with the increased crowds and in 1931 it was replaced with a much simpler struc-ture. To the west of the pier below Pier Hill stood

**113**   Marine Parade in 1924, looking towards the Kursaal.

the Floral Hall, a concert and entertainment venue destroyed by fire in 1937.

The town's first motorised lifeboat, the *Greater London*, was introduced in 1928 and a new lifeboat house and slipway was built at the pierhead in 1935.

The centenary of the pier, first erected in 1830, was rather bizarrely celebrated in 1935 as it was then 100 years since it had first appeared on Admiralty charts.

The reclamation of land on the shoreline either side of the pier increased the seafront area and inspired the creation of the 'sunken gardens'. The western garden featured such rides as 'electrically driven children's motor cars' and the 'Peter Pan Railway' (forerunner of Peter Pan's Playground). The eastern one, incorporating the old waterchute

basin, tended to concentrate on swimming and bathing.

Away from the seafront one of the great attractions of this period was the cinema. The *Rivoli*, *Gaumont*, *Regal*, *Gem* and *Strand* resulted from a frenzy of cinema building, some seating up to 2,000 people. Amongst the most popular was *Garon's Imperial Bioscope* in the High Street, facing Warrior Square. Amongst the most prestigious were the *Astoria* (built on the site of Luker's High Street brewery and later to become the 'old' Odeon) and the *Ritz* (in Grove Terrace near the *Palace Hotel*), both of which opened in 1935. Many of the suburbs also had cinemas.

Another growing attraction was football. Southend United moved in the 1919-20 season to the Kursaal, and became one of the founder members of the new

Third Division South, which replaced the Southern League in 1920-21. In 1934 the club moved to a new football/greyhound stadium in Grainger Road (now the Greyhound Retail Park). This represented another advance in team fortunes, but there were complaints that the dog track around the pitch led to a loss of atmosphere.

The town was drawing millions of visitors per annum by the late 1930s and in 1942 the author, Arthur Mee, could write of Southend as 'the Londoner's seaside, a crowded pleasure place, noisy and happy as a medieval fair ground'.

## Business

With all these visitors, business was positively booming. Well established firms such as Brightwell's, Garon's and Jones' were complemented by Owen

114   The opening of the pier extension (eastern arm) in 1929 by H.R.H. Prince George.

115   The western sunken garden and pier from the air, 1923.

**116** Advertisements for the *Strand* cinema, 1921 — one of a number of cinemas in the town in the inter-war period.

**117** Southend High Street, looking south towards the railway bridge in 1924.

**118**   The new General Hospital, c.1932.

Wallis (ironmongers) and J. F. Dixon, whose Victoria Circus store, several times extended, became one of the town's best-known businesses. On the diagonally opposite corner of the Circus, where Garon's had premises, a new Victoria Arcade shopping complex was growing up. Dixon's, Garon's, the Technical College and the *Hotel Victoria* made Victoria Circus a real focal point.

Factories were also being built. In 1930 the electrics, plastics and radio manufacturer, E. K. Cole Ltd (EKCO), set up in Priory Crescent, moving from its original home in Leigh. EKCO, the town's largest employer at this time, went on to become one of the best-known names in radio and television in the inter- and immediate post-war periods.

**Emergency Services**

The advent of County Borough status in 1914 gave Southend its own police force (separate from Essex Police).

The incorporation of Leigh into the Borough in 1913 similarly strengthened the fire service, and the hitherto Southend and Leigh brigades merged into one. The service was by now operating motorised fire appliances and, with stations in Tylers Avenue (Southend) and Elm Road (Leigh), there was good, modern coverage across the Borough.

The first ambulances appeared during the First World War.

**A New Hospital**

Despite considerable expansion, Southend was still principally served by the Southend Victoria Hospital in Warrior Square, by now some 40 years old. This had been supplemented for several years by the Borough Sanatorium (later called Westcliff Hospital) and Rochford Hospital (known for a time as Southend Municipal Hospital), but there was a growing realisation that on their own they would be inadequate if the town continued to expand.

The Southend Victoria Hospital, still maintained by voluntary subscriptions, had fewer than 100 beds for a population of well over 100,000. It had been enlarged several times since opening, but, apart from financial constraints, there was no land for further expansion. By the mid-1920s it was decided that the best solution would be to build a new hospital somewhere else in the town.

In 1926 the former Southend MP, Viscount Elveden (formerly Rupert Guinness and later to become the Earl of Iveagh), generously offered a site of 12 acres on Prittlewell Chase, plus a substantial sum of his own money towards the construction of a new hospital. With donations from Edward Cecil Jones and Alderman Albert Martin, the fund-raising campaign got off to a flying start.

One of the most successful fund-raising methods was Southend Carnival, established for this purpose in 1926 (though carnivals had taken place in the

**119**   Eastwood church — the historic centre of Eastwood parish.

town several times before). It is still going strong some 75 years later. Arthur Mee, writing in 1942, commented that 'those who would see Southend as it loves to see itself should come to the carnival in August and join the quarter of a million who watch the three mile long procession'.

The foundation stone for the new hospital was laid by the Duchess of York (now the Queen Mother) on 12 November 1929. The deputy mayor, Alderman R.H. Thurlow-Baker, and the Bishop of Chelmsford were also in attendance.

The new Southend General Hospital was opened on 26 July 1932 by, appropriately, Viscount Elveden (by now the Earl of Iveagh). The Earl and his wife, the Countess of Iveagh (formerly Lady Gwendolen Onslow and successor to the Earl as Southend MP), were both given the Freedom of the Borough in recognition of their services to the hospital cause and their parliamentary representation for the town.

The first patients were admitted from the old Southend Victoria Hospital in November. Many of the wards in the new 235-bed building were named after the leading hospital supporters.

## Three More Acquisitions

By the late 1920s, barely 15 years after Leigh had been incorporated into the Borough, councillors were again looking to extend the boundaries. Hadleigh, the next parish west from Leigh, was showing a lot of interest and sent along a deputation along to put their case. There was also talk of parts of Rayleigh and/or Thundersley being included.

In the end, however, councillors opted for three complete parishes to the north and east of the town (with a few negotiated boundary adjustments in two of them). These changes, introduced in 1933, brought Eastwood, South Shoebury and North Shoebury into the Borough. The number of wards was increased to 13 and the number of aldermen and councillors representing them to 13 and 39 respectively.

## Eastwood

Part of the old Eastwood parish had been included in Southend Borough with Leigh in 1913 and it was perhaps not surprising that the rest of it would be annexed. This duly took place in 1933, though in the event, as part of a swap-deal with Rochford Rural District Council, the northern parts of the parish, abutting the River Roach and north of Warners Bridge towards the *Horse & Groom*, were retained by the latter authority.

Unlike Leigh, which shared Southend's tramway network, coastline and progressive outlook, Eastwood was something of a backwater, having almost nothing in common with the growing seaside resort. An inland, almost entirely rural parish, with a small population, it had more in common historically with Rayleigh or Rochford (to the west and north-east respectively) than with Southend. What it did offer, though, was plenty of land.

Eastwood was a long narrow parish, running west to east along Rayleigh Road, White House Road and Eastwoodbury Lane, bordered by Rayleigh in the west, the River Roach in the north, Prittlewell in the east and Leigh in the south. Its historic centre was towards the eastern end of the parish, near the parish church of St Laurence and All Saints. Here was the manor house, Eastwood Bury, and several ancient cottages, most of which have disappeared. The church, however, survives largely unaltered from its 11th-century form. Its most notable vicar, Samuel Purchas (*c.*1610), was a travel writer of some repute.

Apart from the church, other surviving buildings of note include the 16th-century Cockethurst Farm (whose one-time owner, John Vassal, was a part-owner of the *Mayflower*), Bellhouse Farm (now the *Bellhouse* pub) and Blatches Farm (originally in Eastwood but 'moved' with the 1933 boundary changes into Hawkwell).

The parish name comes from its situation on the eastern side of the wood (and parkland) of Rayleigh. The western part of the parish was originally in Rayleigh Park – a large open area used by kings for hunting. The eastern part may have been part of a similar Rochford Park.

Like Prittlewell and Southchurch, Eastwood was once in the ownership of the Rich/Warwick families, having passed via the Crown from Robert Fitzwimarc and Sweyn.

## South Shoebury

By 1933 the old parish of South Shoebury had evolved into a modern town, run since the mid-1890s by Shoeburyness Urban District Council. The transformation from rural parish to small town was sparked by the arrival in 1849 of the Government's Board of Ordnance, which purchased land there for a firing range. Over the next two decades this expanded into a complete military complex, with horseshoe-shaped barracks, a clock tower/gatehouse, a hospital and even a church. The whole complex became known as 'Shoebury Garrison'. From 1889 onwards land was acquired for a larger firing range to the north (actually in North Shoebury parish). This was called 'New Ranges' and the original firing range became 'Old Ranges'.

The original centre of South Shoebury had been around the parish church of St Andrew and neighbouring South Shoebury Hall (both still there), to the west of the Garrison, accessed from the north via North Shoebury Road or, later, along the shore from growing Southend. The name 'Shoebury' means 'a fortified position near a shoe-shaped piece of land'.

Shoebury was held at the time of Domesday Book by Robert Fitzwimarc, the Bishop of Bayeux and others. Like much of the rest of the borough, it later came into the ownership of the Rich/Warwick families. One of the best-known incumbents at South Shoebury church was the Reverend Arthur Dent, rector *c.*1600, whose book *The Plaine Man's Pathway to Heaven* was used by John Bunyan as the model for his *The Pilgrim's Progress*.

The arrival of the Army, however, brought a change of emphasis and two separate but linked South Shoebury communities sprang up. One – 'the village', centred around the High Street – was a place for commerce, with shops conveniently located at the barracks entrance. The other – Cambridge Town (named after one-time Army Commander-in-Chief, the Duke of Cambridge) – became a residential centre, a sort of dormitory town to the west of the barracks around old South Shoebury church and Hall. West

**120**   Church Road, South Shoebury, *c.*1930, roughly at the time when the parish was incorporated into Southend.

Road ultimately became the shopping area for Cambridge Town. Population figures for South Shoebury show a massive jump following the military's arrival, increasing ten-fold between 1851 and 1861. Many of the new residents were 'outsiders' and the village gained an unexpected cosmopolitan atmosphere.

The name 'Shoeburyness' (instead of South Shoebury) was first brought into widespread use in Army correspondence (their lands were situated at the ness (headland) of the parish) and this soon replaced 'South Shoebury' as the common name for the area.

In the 1930s there were plans to develop the town's East Beach as a resort, but this never happened. With the Army blocking the best beaches, most excursion traffic ended up on Shoebury

Common, to the west of South Shoebury towards Thorpe Bay. A holiday camp was set up to the south of South Shoebury Hall.

Several old South Shoebury buildings lie hidden behind the military fences, whilst the Red House (1673) is more easily visible at the junction of Elm and Wakering Roads.

**North Shoebury**

In contrast to South Shoebury, the boundary with which was roughly Elm Road, North Shoebury was still largely rural by the time in 1933 of its acquisition by Southend. Its historic centre, around the 13th-century parish church of St Mary the Virgin and neighbouring North Shoebury Hall (the latter now demolished), was sufficiently remote from the military development (the New Ranges

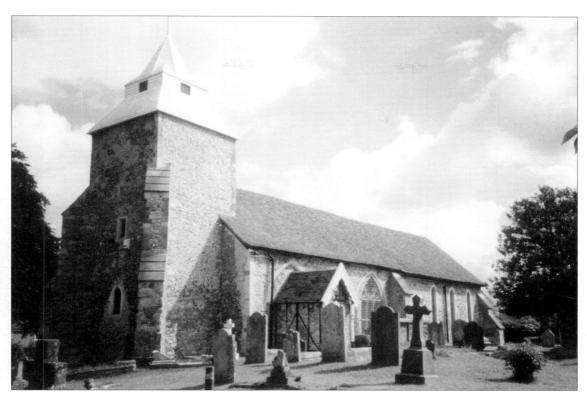

**121**   North Shoebury church.

excepted) to be out of reach of South Shoebury's expansion. The railway line, running east–west between the two parishes, also acted as a barrier to northward development.

Like South Shoebury, North Shoebury was originally accessed from the north, down North Shoebury Road. The junction with Poynters Lane and what is now Bournes Green Chase – 'Parsons Corner' – became something of a local focal point, and North Shoebury Post Office and other buildings were set up there. Several of these buildings survived development and were restored in the 1990s and converted into the *Angel* inn. Nearby, North Shoebury House in Poynters Lane was the birthplace of Rochford Hundred historian Philip Benton and is marked with a plaque. Several other old buildings survive, including New Farm and the White House. One of the 16th-century barns of old North Shoebury Hall also survives – as the *Parsons Barn* public house.

**122**   The medieval Fox Hall Farmhouse – originally in Shopland parish but incorporated into Southend during the 1933 boundary changes.

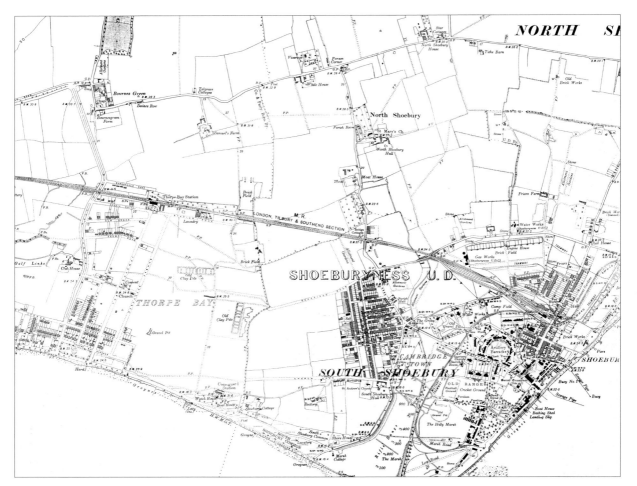

**123** An extract from the 3rd Edition Ordnance Survey map of 1923, showing the eastern side of the borough. Thorpe Bay is a small, if independent, community, linked to Southend to the west via the seafront road and the Thorpe Hall Avenue/Southchurch Boulevard route. Bournes Green survives as a separate hamlet. The map shows the boundary between Southend borough and Shoebury to the east. North and South Shoebury were not incorporated into the borough until 1933. South Shoebury is fairly well developed, whilst North Shoebury is still totally rural.

Not all of the old North Shoebury parish was included in Southend Borough during the 1933 boundary changes – part of it was retained by Rochford Rural District Council and added to the latter's Great Wakering parish.

The parish of Shopland was also affected by the boundary changes. Here Fox Hall Farmhouse (thought to have 14th-century origins) was moved into the borough. This has been restored in recent years under the ownership of the neighbouring Essex Golf Complex.

**Post-acquisition Expansion**

The acquisition of these parishes made much more land available for Southend's expansion. The development of the Thorpedene Estate off Caulfield Road brought Shoebury and Thorpe Bay closer together, while in Eastwood streets began to be laid out between Eastwood Road North and Rayleigh Road.

Another big development of the 1930s was around Cuckoo Corner, when streets were laid out on the old Earls Hall Estate (Earls Hall Avenue, Mayfield Avenue, etc.). The construction of a more

**124** The Earls Hall Estate from the air, showing Earls Hall and Mayfield Avenues, 1931.

direct road to Rochford (Manners Way) in the late 1930s opened up land for Oaken Grange Drive, Byrne Drive and Hampton Gardens. The Somerset Gardens Estate, off Bridgewater Drive, also began to emerge.

Even before the incorporation of three new parishes, traffic had grown to such an extent that Southend Council had already decided that 'the time has now arrived when the northern carriageway of the London to Southend Arterial Road should be completed'. This took until 1939 (the looming war and a Council deputation to the Ministry of Transport influencing its completion) and by then people were beginning to think about using some of the newly acquired

Eastwood land abutting the road for industrial premises, an idea that would be revived after the war.

Eastwood and South Shoebury both brought schools with them (though more were proposed) and received in return electricity and police boxes. Shoebury had a gas works (soon to pass to the Gas, Light & Coke Company) and a fire station (which immediately became a sub-station to Southend) and quickly gained a new police station as well. As in Leigh, several houses 'unfit for human habitation' were demolished following acquisition.

By the end of the 1930s Southend's population was rapidly rising towards the 150,000 mark.

**125**   Southend Airport, pictured *c*.1953.

**A New Nature Reserve**

As the population rose and more and more virgin land was swallowed, the first big local environmental campaign appeared.

In the west of the borough, beyond the Highlands Estate, Belfairs and Hadleigh Great Woods were gradually being eroded by development. The construction of Belfairs golf course there in the 1920s also led to the removal of some trees and there were those who feared that the whole lot would soon disappear. Southend was not well-blessed with woodland and even the best bit of this area – the Great Wood – was over the boundary in Hadleigh (administered by now by the Benfleet Urban District Council (B.U.D.C.)).

In 1936 a proposal to acquire the Great Wood for a nature reserve was rejected as being too costly, even with B.U.D.C. and Essex County Council

(E.C.C.) agreeing to contribute to the expenses. The following year a deputation from the recently formed South Essex Natural History Society was received by the Council. Their pleas were at first ignored, but later in 1937, following intense public pressure, the Council took the decision, with funding from B.U.D.C. and E.C.C. as promised, to acquire the wood and open it as a reserve. This was a momentous decision, resulting in the establishment in 1938 of the first nature reserve in the county and one of the first in the country. The reserve, and the contiguous Belfairs Woods, remain a popular local amenity to this day.

**The Airport**

Another amenity created at this time was Southend Municipal Airport. Built on land to the north of Eastwoodbury Lane and the west of Warners

**126**   The Auxiliary Fire Service at Kent Elms, *c*.1940.

Bridge (originally in the old Eastwood parish but with the 1933 boundary changes now largely in Rochford), it occupied an old training and fighter defence station that had been used by the Royal Flying Corps during the First World War.

Acquired by the Corporation in 1933, it was officially opened in 1935 and the newly-formed Southend Flying Club took over its day-to-day management. Regular flights to Rochester were soon established, but the planes had barely got off the ground before a major barrier to further development raised its head …

**The Second World War**

The Second World War had a much greater effect on Southend than the First. Air warfare had advanced considerably in the intervening 20 years, making aerial bombardment a much greater threat. Within easy reach of the Continent and close to London, Southend was a key target for both airborne and seaborne attacks.

As early as 1935 the Borough Council set up an Air Raid Precautions (A.R.P.) Committee, in line with Home Office instructions. An emergency fire brigade was established in 1938 and plans for the complete 'blackout' of the town at night were underway. By summer 1939 cellars in public buildings were being strengthened for use as air-raid shelters and gas masks for babies and children were being ordered. Anderson shelters were introduced and plans were afoot to dam Prittle Brook to create reservoirs of water for the Fire Brigade.

At the outbreak of war in September 1939 the airport and pier were both requisitioned. Gun emplacements appeared at Thorpe Bay and Belfairs and air-raid shelters were set up at schools and in the tramway Boulevards. Buildings were sandbagged, fire watchers enlisted, air-raid drills practised and a local Home Guard established. Parts of Southchurch, Chalkwell and Belfairs Parks were ploughed up for food production to reduce reliance on supplies from America.

On 22 November 1939 the first (and only) serious attack was made on Southend Pier, by now under the control of the Thames and Medway Naval

**127** Eastern Esplanade, showing (left) the two surviving blocks from the Second World War seafront defences. There were originally over 1,800 such blocks and accompanying barbed wire along the seafront to guard against invasion.

Control Service as 'HMS Leigh' and closed to the public. The pier was undamaged, but two unexploded magnetic mines discovered in the mud off Shoebury after the attack were examined and gave clues to the construction of this new type of weapon. Royal Terrace and the *Palace Hotel* were also occupied by the military.

The River Thames was the key to the defence of London and the pier played an integral role in the protection of the river during the war. Gun emplacements and searchlights were set up there and every movement of shipping was logged. Convoy conferences were held at the pierhead and by 1945 over 3,000 convoys (comprising over 80,000 ships) had been organised. Downriver, between Shoebury and Kent, a gigantic boom was set up across the mouth of the river to control shipping. Part of it (an updated version built during the Cold War) remains to this day. Further out in

the estuary, concrete forts were built on the Nore, Red and Shivering Sands as a front line of defence. Some of these also survive – they can be seen (through binoculars) from East Beach in Shoebury.

In late May and early June 1940 many local boats were used in the 'Little Ships' armada which went to Dunkirk to rescue British soldiers. Vessels which took part included the Southend lifeboat, *Greater London*, and several Leigh fishing boats, one of which, the *Renown*, never made it back.

As the war began to intensify, the government declared Southend an evacuation area and the town's schoolchildren were evacuated to the Midlands. On Sunday 2 June 1940 school after school was ferried to the town's two main railway stations and over 7,000 children were dispatched to other parts of the country. Many adults left too and Southend became something of a ghost town, the population dropping dramatically. Shops were boarded up and

**128** Bomb damage in Campbell Road, Westcliff, in 1941. The area was completely redeveloped in the 1970s and the site is now occupied by a school. A recognisable landmark, however, can be seen in the background – St Paul's church in Salisbury Avenue.

many of the empty schools and houses were taken over by soldiers. Southend became a restricted town and concrete anti-tank blocks and barbed wire fences were laid out on the beach the length of the seafront to prevent enemy landings. A large area of Westcliff was later taken over by the Navy and became known as 'HMS Westcliff'.

In summer and autumn 1940 the Battle of Britain was raging and the skies over Southend were filled with planes. Southend Airport, now under the control of the Royal Air Force (successors to the Royal Flying Corps), played a crucial role in the defence of the country. Shoebury Garrison, with its military facilities and weapons-testing capabilities, was another key establishment, whilst local firms such as EKCO provided components for radar and other military equipment.

By 1944 the tide was beginning to turn in the Allies' favour and Southend had one more major

high-profile role to play. Ships for D-Day were assembled in the Thames in late May and early June 1944, along with several components for the floating 'Mulberry' harbours which were to be built on the Normandy beaches. So much traffic built up in the river that space to manoeuvre was tight and there were two high-profile casualties. One of these, a section of Mulberry harbour, ran aground off Thorpe Bay and can still be seen from the Southend shoreline. The other, an American ship, *Richard Montgomery* – packed with explosives – ran aground on the Kent side of the river. (It too remains visible, albeit harder to see from the Southend side.) Some of the explosives were removed shortly after the accident, but many still remain. There are periodically suggestions to remove them, since any explosion is expected to have far-reaching effects even now, but expert opinion has consistently been to leave them where they are.

**129**  One of the most
famous bombings of the
war — that on R.A.
Jones' jeweller's shop in
the High Street in 1942.

**130**   A wartime rescue vehicle, 1943.

1944 also saw the first flying bomb (V1) and rocket (V2) attacks, as Germany fired its parting shots in a war it knew it was losing.

People had been trickling back to the town during the last two or three years of the war and, when it ended, victory was celebrated just as enthusiastically as it was in other towns across Britain.

More than 60 people died from air attacks on Southend. The pier, the airport and the factories played a key role in the defence of the country.

The MP, Alan Herbert, wrote afterwards that Southend now had 'a proud place in England's history'.

# Seven

# Post-War Heyday and Major Change

After the war the Council's hitherto unrelenting expansionist policy was forced to take a back seat, as the immediate post-war period became one of rebuilding, reassessment and consolidation. There were no new parish acquisitions and the development 'footprint' set out in the 1930s was not significantly extended. The population, temporarily reduced by mass evacuation, began to return to its pre-war levels, but the sharp jumps that had been seen since the turn of the century were now replaced by more gradual increases. The 1951 population was 151,000; in 1961 it was 165,000, and it levelled out after that.

**Entertainment**

Southend was at its peak of popularity in the late 1930s; the pier, the Kursaal, the boat trips and the new Illuminations (known as 'The Lights') all pulled

**131** Lord Broadbridge at the controls of the new 1949 green-and-cream pier trains during the opening ceremony.

**132**   Proclamation of the accession of Queen Elizabeth II in 1952.

in the crowds. When peace resumed in 1945 visitors started to return. The old pier trains were by now nearly 60 years old and had to be replaced. The new green and cream trains, launched on 13 April 1949 by former Lord Mayor of London, Lord Broadbridge, provided covered transport on the pier for the first time. Visitors to the pier alone that year rose to over three million.

The Illuminations were at their height in the 1950s and early 1960s, complementing ever-popular Kursaal rides such as the water chute, bowl slide and Wall of Death. Traffic congestion was a major issue every summer. On one Saturday in 1951 an incredible 2,000 coaches brought sightseers to the town. The Council used every available space for parking and traffic was directed to sites the length of the seafront and even as far inland as the airport! A carpark at Seaway, just

behind Marine Parade, became a key parking area for visitors.

The 'Kursaal Flyer', a steam train-shaped carnival float, was a popular entry in carnivals throughout the country. Ben Oakley and his orchestra were a popular pier attraction, as was the neighbouring *Golden Hind*, a replica ship filled with waxworks which arrived in the old pier waterchute basin in the late 1940s. At the far end of the pier ships such as the *Royal Eagle*, *Medway Queen* and *Royal Daffodil* continued traditional trips over the water. Ticket kiosks stood below Pier Hill and attractions even included day excursions to France.

Weekly 'Miss Lovely' and annual Carnival Queen competitions were enthusiastically supported, while the national Coronation week in 1953 and local railway service centenary in 1956 provided other occasions for celebration. A model village, a new

**133**   The Cliffs Pavilion, which, due to war and money shortages, took 30 years to complete.

clifftop bandstand and the demolition of the old Prospect Place and Row on Eastern Esplanade all helped with the overall appeal.

Belfairs Nature Reserve was extended, with an additional purchase of over 50 acres, and a new 'Garden of Memory' (dedicated in 1952) was established in Chalkwell Park in commemoration of those who had fought and died in the war. In 1954 Edward Cecil Jones donated some land to the east of his father's Jones Memorial Ground in Eastern Avenue as a Youth Commemoration Ground for teenagers and also in memory of those who had fought in the war.

In music, the Beatles and the Rolling Stones visited Southend in the 1960s.

The biggest issue in entertainment in the immediate post-war period was the provision of a purpose-built theatre and concert venue – the Cliffs Pavilion. There had been talk of such a venue since the 1920s and in the early 1930s the Council purchased land at Shorefields for the new attraction.

Foundations were laid, but lack of money and the advent of war both put paid to any further work. In 1949 the Council's Publicity Committee recommended the completion of the Pavilion as the town's contribution to the 1951 Festival of Britain, but nothing was done and the matter rumbled on throughout the 1950s. In 1959, however, the (1890) pier pavilion was destroyed by fire (it was replaced two years later by a bowling alley) and this provided the necessary impetus. Building work recommenced on the pre-war foundations and the long-awaited Cliffs Pavilion finally opened in 1964. The town's first purpose-built art gallery – the Beecroft (named after its primary local advocate, Walter G. Beecroft) – had opened in premises opposite the Cliffs Pavilion site in 1953.

In 1969 the Warrior Square swimming pool opened, replacing the Westcliff Swimming Baths. These saw one season (1970) of performing dolphins before going into private ownership as the Westcliff Leisure Centre.

**134**   Northumberland Avenue on the low-lying seafront during the floods of 1953.

### Industry

There had been discussions during the war about whether Southend should continue to concentrate so heavily on entertainment or whether investment should be made to attract revenue-generating light industry. The EKCO factory had proved a huge success and there were those who thought that others should follow.

In 1942 Councillor Edward Cecil Jones suggested that a Special Committee should be set up 'for the purpose of drawing up a comprehensive plan for the post-war development of the County Borough as a residential, health and holiday resort, also having in mind the need for light industrial undertakings'. In 1944 the committee produced its recommendations, known as the 'Miles Report' after the Mayor, Alderman William Miles. This report formed the basis of Southend's development for the next 25-30 years.

By 1947 the Council was looking to open an industrial estate at the western end of the borough in Eastwood, close to the A127 and easily accessible by road from London. They put in a new road to serve it and the Progress Road Industrial Estate was born. Others would soon follow.

A land deal in 1950 with the North Thames Gas Board (successors to the Gas, Light & Coke Company) resulted in the latter moving to Progress Road. In return, the Council acquired former Gas Board land at Roots Hall, one-time home of Southend United. The football club wanted to move from its Grainger Road stadium and in 1952 a deal was done. The site needed a bit of work – the area had largely been used as a rubbish tip – but with a bit of effort, much of it from the supporters' club, it was transformed into one of the best small grounds in the country when it opened in 1955. Southend United was back home.

## 1953 Flood

In 1953 the highest tide in living memory carried floodwaters over the sea defences and into the low-lying seafront area of the town. Southchurch Park, Peter Pan's Playground and parts of Leigh and Shoebury were all affected.

Plans for flood defences to be raised across the borough were soon in place.

## A Period of Consolidation

As houses were rebuilt after the war and the undeveloped gaps between them were filled, so the infrastructure was also improved.

The Prittlewell Chase/Kenilworth Gardens/Blenheim Chase route was completed (over a period of years) from Fairfax Drive to Belfairs (only sections of it had been constructed pre-war) and the area around Blenheim (formerly part of the Brickhouse Farm estate) was gradually developed as a consequence. Traffic lights, roundabouts and pedestrian crossings sprung up across the town. Victoria Circus – which was becoming very busy – was remodelled in 1951-2 with a one-way system in Southchurch Road and Warrior Square. Other one-way systems soon followed.

The only truly new areas to be developed in this period were the outlying areas of Eastwood (various streets off The Fairway and Rayleigh Road) and Southchurch (around Newington and Archer Avenues). The population of Eastwood in particular grew noticeably at this time. The Eastern Avenue extension from Hamstel Road to Bournes Green was complete by the early 1970s. The land between Thorpe Bay and Shoebury was also further developed, drawing the two settlements ever closer together until they finally met at Maplin Way. There was also some development of North Shoebury at this time in the Eagle Way and Constable Way areas.

New schools – including Prince Avenue, Blenheim, Temple Sutton, Fairway, Belfairs, Thomas More, Cecil Jones (named after the councillor) and others – were opened between the end of the war and the early 1970s. Southend High School for Girls gained a new home in Southchurch Boulevard and in 1952 Brewery Road School was renamed 'Porters Grange'. Old schools such as the London Road School and Southchurch's National School were closed, to be followed later by Hamlet Court. Youth Centres, clinics and other community buildings such as the crematorium (dedicated in 1953) all appeared.

In 1949 the Chief Fire Officer complained that duplicate street names were causing problems in identifying the locations of fires. This had arisen following Southend's acquisition of other areas (Southend, Leigh and Shoebury all had 'High Streets', for example) and it was agreed that there would be no street name duplication from now on.

'Nationalisation' (in its broadest sense) was a feature of the immediate post-war period, and gas and electricity services were consolidated into national (if regionally run) organisations. The fire service had become a national operation in 1941 as a result of the war (though, as a County Borough, Southend retained a brigade until 1974). The 1946 National Health Service Act (effective from 1948) took hospitals out of local authority control and in the latter year Southend's two railway lines came under the same company for the first time – the new British Rail. The two main stations took on their current names of 'Southend Victoria' and 'Southend Central' shortly afterwards. Both lines were soon electrified – Southend Victoria in 1956 and Southend Central in 1962. In 1951 bus transport was reorganised under the British Transport Commission. In 1949 the Council had to move its elections from November to May – another trend towards national unity.

In Parliament, Henry Channon, son-in-law of the Countess of Iveagh, was succeeded at a by-election in January 1959 by his son, Paul, continuing a remarkable sequence of election successes by the family.

## Leigh

There were several proposals for grandiose schemes at Leigh from the 1940s to the 1960s as the Council took the approach (as it did elsewhere in the town) of 'out with the old and in with the new'. Several historic buildings in the Old Town High Street were demolished under a Prittlewell-style 'Improvement Scheme'.

Leigh Marshes and neighbouring Two Tree Island were particular favourites; a tip was set up there and various plans were proposed for yacht

**135** Southchurch Road, *c.*1951. Yes, the lorry has crashed into the lamppost!

**136**   The 'Road to the West' bridge at Leigh-on-Sea, intended as an outlet for a seafront route from Southend, which was never built.

marinas. There were also proposals for the relocation of the historic cocklesheds and, perhaps most controversially, for a new 'Road to the West' from Central Southend, which would run along Chalkwell and Leigh foreshores, through the ancient High Street (hence the building demolition) and out via a new bridge over the railway line at the suburb's western end. The bridge was actually built – it replaced the congested (now gone) level-crossing opposite the *Ship* as the main access point into the Old Town – but the rest of the scheme was opposed so vigorously by local people that it was shelved in the mid-1970s.

### The Airport

The airport was released from military service into Council ownership after the war and from the late 1940s there was talk of expansion. Holiday and freight traffic (including car ferries) was increasing

and entrepreneurs such as Freddie Laker were showing an interest. The old Eastwood Bury manor house was initially acquired for use by airport staff, but was demolished in 1954.

The west side of the airport was the easiest to develop and in 1964 the Council decided to put in a new estate road – Aviation Way. This provided access to the airfield and also made new land available for industrial purposes.

Arguably the most significant campaign of the period was for the extension of the runway. Concrete runways had replaced grass in the mid-1950s as planes had grown heavier, but the runway length prevented the landing of larger aircraft and was seen as a restriction to the potential economic profitability of the town. Matters came to a head in 1967 when a government minister decided against extension. This came as a massive blow to the Council and they were forced to concentrate in-

**137**   St Christopher's Special School in Victoria Avenue in 1959. This was chosen as the site for the new police station as part of the Civic Centre scheme. The area has been completely transformed, but the public library (now Southend Central Museum) can be seen at the top right of the photograph.

stead on developing Aviation Way, including the construction of a motel, discotheque and Historic Aircraft Museum. They also took the opportunity (in 1969) to demolish some old buildings at the western end of the main runway near Eastwood church.

**Maplin Airport**

Plans for the airport were greatly affected in the late 1960s and early 1970s by proposals to build a new airport on Maplin Sands, east of Shoeburyness. Simultaneous proposals for a seaport there led to 'Maplin' being a huge issue in south-east Essex. Southend Borough Council was initially broadly in favour of the proposals – subject to confirmation of the effects on Southend airport and the local road network – but public opposition, especially from conservationists worried about the effect on seabirds, ultimately saw the scheme(s) abandoned.

By 1974 the Council was admitting that it was 'horrified at the appalling environmental consequences which the proposals would have on the area'.

**Major Change**

The 1960s and early 1970s was to be a period of major change in Southend, as several long-planned schemes (and a few new ones) finally came to fruition. Much of the Victorian and Edwardian town was swept away and it can clearly be seen in retrospect that this was a watershed in the town's development.

**The Town Hall**

There had been plans for a new Town Hall in Southend since the late 19th century. The Municipal Buildings in Clarence Road had served the town well, but by the late 1950s accommodation was at

**138**    The Queen Mother opening the new Council Chamber at the Civic Centre in October 1967.

bursting point. The Council's various departments were housed all over the town and there was a clear need to consolidate them on one site.

The police and courts services were also running out of space and it was decided to apply for a complete 'Civic Centre' with a Council chamber, offices for Council workers, a police station, cells and a courtroom, and perhaps a new college building, a new central library and maybe even a fire station. The site chosen was Victoria Avenue.

In the event, all were constructed except the fire station, which moved from its Tylers Avenue home in 1964 to new premises in Sutton Road. The Leigh fire station also moved – to the site of Brickhouse Farm (unsuccessfully suggested for

preservation in 1961) – where it was opened in March 1969, a few months after its first occupation.

The Civic Centre scheme was a big operation and its opening was organised in the following stages:

The police station opened in March 1962; the courthouse in February 1966. The Civic Suite and office block (usually referred to these days as the 'Civic Centre') were opened in October 1967 by the Queen Mother. The Council chamber was built to accommodate 90 councillors. (There were 48 councillors and 16 aldermen at the time, following an increase in 1955 – the year of the town's first female Mayor, Constance Leyland – caused by the reorganisation and addition of three new wards: Blenheim, Southbourne and Temple Sutton.) The

**139** The new public library, opened in 1974 to replace the old one (now Southend Central Museum), pictured in the background.

**140** The Queen Mother outside the new Civic Centre in October 1967, showing the new Victoria Avenue dualling.

office block – 14 storeys high – set 'the pattern for the new skyline' of the town. A registry office was also opened.

The new College of Technology, behind the tower block in Carnarvon Road, was fully operational by 1971. A supplementary college building had been provided in the late 1950s in London Road and this was retained, but the 1902 Technical College, for so long a focal point of the town, was demolished 'amid considerable controversy' and 'with indecent and unnecessary haste'. The old Municipal Buildings, police station and fire station were also demolished and all four sites were designated for car-parking.

The new Central Library was not ready until 1974, when it opened on the site of a bowling green just north of the original library. The latter building was retained, reopening in 1981 as Southend Central Museum.

## Victoria Avenue

The relocation of the town's administration to Victoria Avenue helped to establish the road as the new business district and its western side became an area of privately owned office blocks.

In 1960 the Council received news that H.M. Customs & Excise were proposing to relocate their Accounting and Statistical functions to Victoria Avenue and Customs later became one of the town's biggest employers. Baryta, Carby, Coleman and Portcullis Houses (office blocks) all opened in the mid-1960s, followed by Alexander House in 1972.

Victoria Avenue over the years had become a fashionable residential street, with big houses and gardens in an atmosphere of exclusivity. All this was swept away, however, in the new order, along with properties in Baxter Avenue behind, to make way for the new buildings and their associated car parks.

The Civic Centre/offices scheme included the dualling of Victoria Avenue, completed in stages between Victoria Circus and Cuckoo Corner. The centuries-old view from the south towards Prittlewell church was now obscured by tower blocks. Prittlewell was no longer thought of as a distinct place – it was just another part of Southend.

A new public park – Churchill Gardens – was opened north of the Civic Centre in 1966 on the site of a former brickworks sandpit.

## The Ring Road

Perhaps the largest scheme of the 1960s was for a Ring Road around the town centre. Traffic had dramatically increased since the war and the Council recognised the need to cater for it if the streets were not to become grid-locked. The town centre one-way scheme of 1951-2 had been useful, but cars and pedestrians still intermingled in the busy High Street. The construction of a Ring Road – and the subsequent pedestrianisation of the High Street – would provide an adequate road system and would separate shoppers and traffic once and for all.

The Ring Road scheme was a major undertaking. It was to begin in the London Road to the west of the town, near the old tramway depot, where a new roundabout would be built. It would then head north-east through Dowsett Avenue to Victoria Avenue at another new roundabout. It would then go east to Porters, where another roundabout (with underpass) was required, and then south through existing streets (Porters Grange Avenue, Bankside, Corsham Road and Darnley Road) to the Seaway car-park. A new roundabout there would send a spur road east to Woodgrange Drive, whilst the main Ring Road would continue to the west, probably through Alexandra Street, crossing under the High Street and turning north somewhere around Park Street to complete the loop at the London Road. The scheme would require the demolition of hundreds of houses and several business premises, with civil engineering on a scale hitherto unseen in the town, not to mention all the accompanying traffic chaos. The 1962 electrification of the Fenchurch Street railway line provided some impetus for reconstruction (most of the bridges on the line had to be raised) and the widening of Bankside bridge on the east side of the Ring Road was actually started as part of this work.

When the Ring Road was first proposed in 1955, 'the completion of a proposal of such magnitude could not obviously be envisaged for very many years'. In the end, only about half of it was built – from London Road to Seaway. The western half,

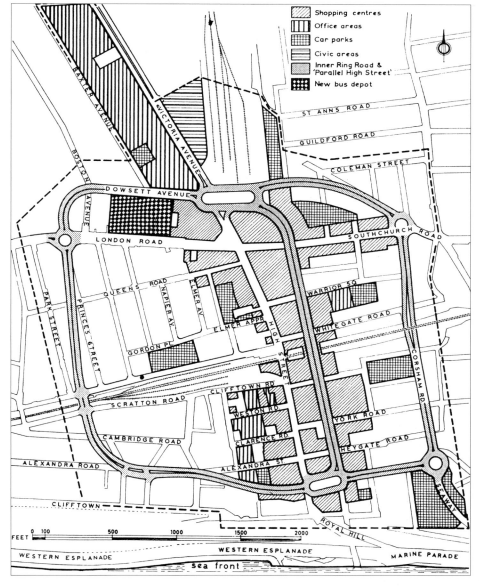

**141** A map from 1960 showing the route of the proposed Ring Road and accompanying Parallel High Street. Only the north and east (top and right) sides of the Ring Road were built. The Parallel High Street (Chichester Road) was built in a different format from the one envisaged here. The south and west sides of the Ring Road were formally abandoned in the late 1970s on cost and environmental heritage grounds.

through Cliff Town – soon to be designated a conservation area – was too difficult and expensive, though the Park Street railway bridge was reconstructed in 1959 (during railway electrification) in preparation.

The Ring Road that was built was constructed in sections: the northern part and Bankside bridge in the late 1960s; the Porters Grange underpass (with a new link to Sutton Road) and the eastern

section in the mid-1970s. The whole length was renamed 'Queensway' in honour of The Queen's Silver Jubilee in 1977.

The Ring Road totally changed the face of the 1870s Porters Town area to the north-east of the High Street – many properties there were compulsorily purchased and several streets completely disappeared. Two-storey Victorian terraces were replaced by four 16-storey tower blocks, named after

**142**  The Ring Road under construction, looking west towards Southend Victoria station in 1966 and showing the new tower blocks (Quantock, Pennine, etc.).

**143**  Park Street railway bridge, which was widened to incorporate the proposed west side of the Ring Road (see map). The west side was never built and the bridge now looks far too wide for everyday traffic.

**144**   Porters Grange underpass nearing completion in 1977.

famous ranges of hills (Pennine, Quantock, etc.). More residential towerblocks would follow elsewhere, notably off Balmoral Road, where war-damaged Campbell Road and several neighbouring streets were completely removed.

Even the hospital gained a towerblock – a new group of wards, opened by Princess Anne in 1971.

**Pedestrianisation and the Parallel High Street**
The construction of the first phases of the Ring Road took traffic out of the town centre and by the late 1960s it was possible to start pedestrianising the High Street. The top end, from Victoria Circus to Warrior Square, was first. The second section, from Warrior Square to Whitegate Road, followed in the mid-1970s.

Another aspect of town-centre redevelopment connected to the Ring Road and pedestrianisation was the construction of a 'Parallel High Street', to the east of the existing one. This would follow the

line of Milton Street and Warrior Square and link up with Grover Street to the south. It would necessitate the construction of a new railway bridge, but this could be accommodated while all the other bridge construction work was going on (though in the event the bridge was not completed until the mid-1970s).

Chichester Road, as the new route became called (it was mooted at the time of yachtsman Sir Francis Chichester's knighthood), would increase the shopping frontage and also provide rear access to shops now in the pedestrianised area.

The complete route opened in the late 1970s. A new bus station was built at the Chichester Road/ York Road junction c.1974.

Marks & Spencer extended their building to the new road, as did Keddie's, who also opened a big tower block (Maitland House). Keddie's new 'Supa Save' store, facing Warrior Square, was the town's first proper supermarket in 1960.

**145** Southend High Street from the new Civic Centre, *c*.1966. The first stage of pedestrianisation has begun and the first stage of the Ring Road (bottom) has been built. The Technical College is still there (front right). The cranes are out for the Hammerson development (left).

**146** The newly pedestrianised top end of the High Street, *c*.1968. Note the Dixon's showcases – a classic 1960s feature, removed in the 1970s after persistent vandalism.

**147** The London Road, *c*.1970, showing the Technical College (left) and the new Hammerson development rising in the background.

On the west side of the High Street (at the top end), shops were now served from behind by a new Farringdon Service Road and what would become the town's first multi-storey shoppers' car park. The latter's construction necessitated the clearance of yet more houses, this time in Farringdon Place itself and in neighbouring Elmer Approach.

This period also said goodbye to some of Southend's oldest and most-loved businesses, many of them still family-run. Amongst the most prominent losses were Brightwell's, Dixon's, the *Hotel Victoria* and the Blue Bird Café.

### Victoria Circus Redevelopment

The principal business activities from the 1940s to the early 1970s centred on the High Street and the neighbouring Talza and Victoria Arcades (a complex of shops and covered alleyways) at the junction of London Road and Southchurch Road. The pedestrianisation of the High Street and the Chichester Road and Ring Road schemes went hand-in-hand with the redevelopment of this area.

In 1964 the Council accepted an offer from the Hammerson group of companies for the redevelopment of the Arcades with a multi-level pedestrian-only shopping centre and a multi-storey car park and office block above. The new centre (now called Victoria Plaza) included an 'imaginative scheme' for an underpass linking the new Ring Road roundabout at Victoria Avenue to Southchurch Road and a small underground bus station, which would supplement the nearby Eastern National bus garage in London Road on the west side of the college. The underpass was named 'Deeping' after the Southend author, Warwick Deeping. The scheme also included a 'shopping bridge' over the Ring Road, which linked the centre to Southend Victoria railway station.

**148**   The Technical College in 1971 during demolition. The Hammerson development is rising behind the billboards on the right, whilst in the background Alexander House is nearing completion. The busy Victoria Circus junction is now fully pedestrianised.

The Hammerson development opened in 1973, and C&A Modes Limited were the main tenants. Not everyone was happy with it; 'part of the character of the town died in the process', wrote one observer.

### Unexpected Developments

These grand schemes were designed to signal a new era in Southend's history, but some unexpected developments were also just around the corner.

First, in 1966, the Council found itself discussing a government plan to remove the borough police force and merge it with the county one. The creation of a separate borough force in 1914 had been against the trend elsewhere at the time, but it had always been popular with local people who feared that its removal would lead to an increase in crime. After lengthy, sometimes heated, discussions, the two forces were merged on 1 April 1969.

Even more significant was a Local Government Commission announcement that it was reviewing local government organisation throughout the country and as a result Southend could lose its cherished County Borough status. Most other local authorities in Essex did not have County Borough powers and Southend feared that their removal would adversely affect the provision of some of the Council's major services. Highways and the fire service, for example, were functions that could be moved to Essex's control.

Similarly, there was a suggestion that the office of alderman should be abolished, as it was undemocratic and open to political abuse.

After long, drawn-out discussions – during which, in 1970, Southend suggested it should take over the whole of Rochford Hundred! – it was decided, to almost universal local displeasure, that the town should lose both its County Borough status and its aldermen and become simply a

'District Council' in common with other similar-sized towns.

On 1 April 1974, after 60 years as a County Borough, Southend was demoted to District status. It was re-promoted to Borough status in name shortly afterwards, but without County Borough powers. The opportunity was taken to realign the wards and reduce councillor numbers and, in 1976, 13 wards were agreed and 39 councillors elected to them. Southend in return gained representation on the County Council for the first time since 1914 – elections for that took place in April 1973.

**Watershed**

The 1960s and early 1970s were planned as a forward-looking milestone in the development of the town. With the war behind it, Southend was progressive and optimistic for the future, and was building roads and services for its people towards a bright new tomorrow.

In retrospect, however, this period did not mark the beginning of a bright new future, but rather the end of an old and cherished heritage, as much-loved buildings, homes and streets were swept away. The development of the town until then had been evolutionary; in the 1960s it was nothing short of revolutionary. The loss of the police force and of County Borough status served only to underline what many people thought as the concrete buildings went up all around them – the end of an era was nigh.

In truth the town's popularity as a holiday resort was already on the wane. Cheap package holidays to Spain were replacing trips to 'The Lights' at Britain's seaside towns and in the late 1960s the pull of Southend's Illuminations began to decline. By 1967, with increasing costs and decreasing visitor numbers, councillors were beginning to scale them down. The hotel trade was suffering and several old and noble hotels, such as the *Palmeira Towers* on Westcliff Esplanade, were subsequently demolished.

Author Marcus Crouch, on a trip around Essex for a 1969 book, had little good to say about Southend, commenting that 'my heart sinks at the thought of all those streets and all those people ...'.

Everyone who lived through the changes seems universally to lament the passing of 'old' Southend. 'It was a much nicer place in the old days,' is a common comment.

Where would Southend go from here?

*Eight*

# Modern Times

In the early evening of 29 July 1976 the pierhead caught fire. Even in the doom and gloom of the era, it stood out as a tragedy. Townsfolk turned up in numbers to watch in horror as the world-famous landmark blazed.

When the smoke cleared, it was evident that serious damage had been done. Most of the amusements had disappeared and the pierhead structure was a tangle of charred wood and twisted metal. It was the town's worst-ever disaster.

**149** A board on Southend pier giving the history of the 1976 pierhead fire. Charred timbers from the event can still be seen behind the sign — 25 years on!

Two years later the pier railway, short of visitors and money following the fire and supposedly structurally unsafe by now, was closed and there were genuine fears that the whole pier would be demolished. Councillors had been struggling to keep it going for a decade or so before the fire and this looked like the final nail in the coffin.

The end was nigh, too, for the Kursaal, Southend's other principal seafront attraction. No longer able to command its previous popularity, it went into decline and by the late 1970s a large part of the site had been sold for housing. The remaining portion closed completely in 1986.

Then there was the *Royal Hotel* ... If any building had symbolised Southend's growth from the 'South End' of Prittlewell to a town in its own right, this was it, but even this was not spared the attentions of developers and there were serious suggestions that it should be demolished ...

## Enough is Enough

By this stage, local people had had enough. They had witnessed large swathes of their heritage being demolished before their very eyes over the previous 15-20 years and the simultaneous threat to the town's three most important historic buildings could not be tolerated.

In 1973 the Southend Society was formed, with the twin aims of saving the *Royal Hotel* from demolition and maintaining the residential character of Cliff Town (still at that stage under threat from the Ring Road scheme). Then a 'Save the Pier' group arose, growing from strength to strength until 1980 when it presented to the Council an 11,000-signature petition against the structure's closure.

The message struck home and in 1986 a restored pier railway sporting new red trains was

**150**   The new (1986) pier trains, with the town in the distance.

formally opened by Princess Anne. This was officially 'the Year of the Pier' and even serious damage by a wayward ship, the *Kingsabbey* – the latest in a long line of ship/pier collisions – could not dampen spirits. Three years later the iron pier's centenary was officially celebrated and a Pier Museum was opened to coincide with it.

**The Town Centre**

The abandonment of the Ring Road scheme in the late 1970s and the increased protection of the *Royal Hotel* and Cliff Town led councillors to review the situation at the southern end of the High Street, where shopping had gone into a decline. They decided to copy the principles of the Hammerson development by creating a self-contained shopping centre offering a variety of stores. The shopping experience had moved on, however, and covered shopping centres were now all the rage. 'The Royals' shopping centre, first proposed in 1978, was born.

Even this development was not without controversy, however – the 1935 *Ritz* cinema, at the corner of Grove Road, was demolished despite conservationists' campaigns. Grove Road itself also disappeared as comprehensive redevelopment completely transformed the area between the southern end of the High Street and Church Road.

This ambitious scheme, occupying a prime High Street/clifftop site, was completed in March 1988. Pedestrianisation of the High Street from the railway bridge to Pier Hill was finished at the same time.

The other major town centre redevelopment of the 1980s was Sainsbury's. There had been proposals for the redevelopment of the Technical College site and the entire London Road frontage west to the new Ring Road roundabout since even before the college was demolished. Schemes had come and gone – the most prominent being a Keddie's proposal for a multi-storey towerblock with shops below, ruled out partly on height grounds under

**151** The Royals shopping centre under construction in June 1987.

**152** The site of the planned Sainsbury's supermarket in London Road as it looked in late 1987.

**153** A photograph of a publicity sales brochure for the Eastwood Lodge estate (off Western Approaches), *c.*1980.

new Civil Aviation Authority restrictions. By 1980, however, everyone had had enough of high-rise concrete and more modest plans were under consideration.

In the end, the college site was left out of the scheme and Sainsbury's instead bought up most of the rest of the London Road premises, replacing them with the largest single-level town centre supermarket Southend had yet seen. It opened in spring 1989.

To the east of Southend Victoria Station, a new Postal Sorting Office was built, replacing the existing one in Tylers Avenue. A new B&Q was constructed next door. Southend Stadium, by now closed for football and dog racing, was redeveloped as the Greyhound Retail Park. All three were open by 1989.

The retail park and D.I.Y. warehouse were visible local symbols of a growing national trend.

**Residential Development**

Large-scale residential development in the 1970s and 1980s continued to be focused in Eastwood (the Western Approaches area) and, increasingly, North Shoebury (land either side of North Shoebury Road). These were the only areas in the borough where large tracts of undeveloped land remained.

Both developments were based around a superstore (Safeway at Eastwood, Asda at North Shoebury), an accompanying parade of shops and a pub, giving them a distinct community focus. North Shoebury church, for so long rurally isolated and now totally alone following the demolition of neighbouring North Shoebury Hall, again became a focal point for the community.

Bournes Green Chase was built and North Shoebury Road improved. Both were left with sufficient land alongside to enable later dualling if required.

**154**   The old and the new together at a rejuvenated North Shoebury. The new (1981) ASDA supermarket provided a community focus for the surrounding housing, in conjunction with the conversion of a barn from North Shoebury Hall into a public house.

Modern housing (individually-styled houses looking part of a corporate whole) became a feature of both areas. Compared with the characterless concrete of the 1960s, the 1980s (and, at North Shoebury, 1990s) housing gave a warm welcome to potential residents. The town's population – in decline for the first time from 1961 to 1981 – began to pick up again. By 1991 it had stabilised at 158,000, whilst the 1998 estimate of 176,000 is the highest in the town's history.

The increasing population was accommodated in part by the conversion into flats of many of the old Edwardian properties in the town. Westborough and Milton were particularly popular choices for this. The Council recognised that there were 'growing environmental problems ... especially where property is being divided into smaller units and on-street parking stress is at a critically high level ...' and began to introduce planning restrictions.

**Business Trends**

The development of new superstores in greenfield sites at Eastwood and North Shoebury mirrored a national trend for 'out-of-town' developments. Two more followed in the 1990s – Waitrose in Eastern Avenue (opened 1994) and Tesco on the A127 (1995). The Tesco scheme included the construction of the town's first purpose-built hotel for almost 100 years – a Brewer's Fayre Travel Inn and pub (*Strawberry Field*, 1998). Perhaps more importantly it also included the construction of a new Southend-Rochford link road (the B1013), built in two stages from the A127 to Hall Road via Eastwoodbury and Cherry Orchard Lanes. The Borough Council had been talking about a 'projected new road ... north from Prince Avenue to Cherry Orchard Lane' since the early 1950s, considering it 'imperative that a main road should be constructed in a northerly direction to provide a

155   An aerial view from 1995 of the new Tesco's supermarket and B1013 Southend–Rochford link road (Nestuda Way, left, with Eastwood church and industrial estates in the distance). The northern section (Cherry Orchard Way), from Eastwood to Rochford, opened the following year — the gap for it can be seen between the warehouses at the top of the picture. The A127 is in the foreground.

156   The new (1995, Cardigan) wing at Southend hospital, built following centralisation of hospital services.

**157** The old Keddie's site in May 1997, cleared and awaiting development as a Tesco Metro store. It changed hands three years later and is now a Gap clothing store.

future outlet for traffic from Southend to the north'. The southern section – Nestuda Way – opened in 1995 (Nestuda being the name for Eastwood in Domesday Book); the northern section – Cherry Orchard Way – in 1996.

Southend Airport also gained a major retail development after the sale of land at Warners Bridge to finance other airport schemes. Management of the airport was transferred from Southend Borough Council to Regional Airports Limited in 1994, when it became 'London Southend Airport'. The airport was seen at the time as 'a large business grown small' – the late-1960s peak of 690,000 passengers per annum had dwindled to 7,000 by 1996. The plan is to increase annual capacity to 300,000 over the coming years.

There were developments, too, in the health service, with the centralisation of Southend and Rochford hospital services at Southend General. The new 1995 Cardigan Wing was the second major redevelopment of the hospital in 25 years. A private (BUPA) hospital opened in Eastern Avenue in the early 1980s.

In the High Street the town said 'goodbye' in the mid-1990s to one of its largest businesses, Keddie's, just a few years after its centenary. The whole country was going through a depression, but it was still a bit of a shock!

**Tourism and Entertainment**

By the late 1980s and early 1990s Southend as a whole was on the up and there was a new wave of optimism and rejuvenation. Nowhere was this more evident than in tourism and entertainment.

Council chiefs recognised that Southend's days as a week-long holiday resort were numbered and concentrated instead on re-attracting the town's original tourist market – the day-tripper.

The Pier Hill Buildings were demolished in the late 1970s to tidy up the pier approach and a series of year-round events was gradually introduced to bring variety and a need for regular re-visits.

The most significant annual event was the Southend Airshow, introduced in 1986. There had been air displays in the town before, dating back to before the First World War, but until now these had usually taken place at the airport. The 1986 May bank holiday show used the tourist-packed seafront as the main flying zone. This move was so successful that Southend Airshow quickly became established as Europe's largest free flying event. The 2001 event pulled in 500,000 visitors.

In 1992 the Borough Centenary was celebrated and Charter Day (19 September) was attended by the Lord Mayor of London, Sir Brian Jenkins, and mayors from several Essex towns. People across the

**158** A flypast during Southend Air Show in May 2001. Over half a million visitors annually are attracted to the town for this event.

town took part and a new Centenary Garden, complete with time capsule, was opened at Priory Park.

Perhaps more importantly, several new permanent attractions appeared. Never Never Land was rejuvenated and a new Victorian-style bandstand was opened on the clifftop above. In December 1992 a revamped Cliffs Pavilion reopened with increased seating capacity. In June 1993 Southend Sea Life Centre opened on Eastern Esplanade, roughly in the vicinity of the long-demolished Methodist Church.

After a decade standing empty, the Kursaal was restored, reopening to a rapturous welcome in May 1998. In 1995 the pier had suffered yet another fire, with the loss of its 1960s bowling pavilion, so

**159** A celebration for the Southend Borough Centenary in 1992, with the windows of Alexander House illuminated in a predetermined pattern.

bowling lanes were provided at the Kursaal as a replacement. A new Kursaal Flyer was also built, appearing in carnivals from 1997 onwards.

A new attraction appeared in the eastern sunken garden – Peter Pan's Adventure Island, which was linked by a new tunnel under the pier to the original Peter Pan's Playground in the western sunken garden. Attractions opened in phases from 1995 onwards. A *Golden Hind* replacement – still occupying the old water chute basin area – was launched in 1998.

Inland, the biggest leisure development of the 1990s was the Garon Leisure Park – a joint venture between the Norman Garon Trust and Southend

**160**   An aerial photograph of the seafront in 1995, taken shortly after the fire at the landward end of the pier (top left). Signs of rejuvenation are in evidence, however, with the new (1993) Sea Life Centre (bottom left) and the beginnings of the construction of Adventure Island in the eastern sunken garden just right of the pier. Towards the bottom of the picture, in the centre, is the abandoned Kursaal, soon to be restored to life.

**161**   The Essex Golf Centre at the new Garon Leisure Park under construction in the early 1990s. Fox Hall Farmhouse can be seen in the lower left of the picture.

Borough Council. Described as 'the most exciting leisure project in more than 40 years in Southend', it covered some 300 acres and included an equestrian centre (just outside the Borough in Shopland), a golf course (at Fox Hall Farm), an athletics track and an indoor Leisure & Tennis Centre. It opened in stages from 1993 to 1996. The new Chase Fitness Centre in Prittlewell Chase opened in 1994, whilst the Warrior Square swimming pool gained a 1990s revamp.

Back in town the old Technical College site was finally built on; in November 1996 a new eight-screen Odeon cinema multiplex opened (now the only cinema in the town). This and a new 'town square', with an accompanying parade of shops and restaurants, gave renewed focus to the Victoria Plaza area.

From 1992 onwards Southend picked up several Britain in Bloom Awards, plus Blue Flags for its beaches (now officially pollution free after some late-1980s controversies) and Green Flags for its parks.

Even Southend United joined the 1990s rejuvenation, gaining promotion in 1991 to what was then the Second Division – the first time in its history the club had reached such dizzy heights.

In 1996 the Council proudly reported that 'everywhere you look, things are happening'. When the Queen visited Victoria Avenue and the seafront in March 1999 she must have been very impressed by what she saw.

## Council

By 1994 things were even looking up for the local authority. The loss of County Borough status in 1974 had not been forgotten and there was still ill-feeling about it in Southend. A Local Government review, however, gave Councils the opportunity to apply for Unitary Authority status (basically County Borough status under another name) and Southend promptly started to make its case. Essex County Council, keen to retain control of all the county's services, took the opposing view.

In the end, after lengthy public consultation and review, Southend won the day and from 1 April 1998 became a Unitary Authority. There was no doubting the tone of the announcement

in the Council's newspaper, the *Civic News*, which described Southend as 'reclaiming from Essex County Council nearly all the powers it had to give up in the 1970s' (education, social services, libraries, highways, traffic management and others).

There was an added bonus for one of the six formerly separate parishes in the borough as Leigh was granted its own Town Council in 1996 in recognition of its strong community identity. Southend was still in overall control, but at least Leigh had some say in its own affairs – for the first time since 1913!

The increase in workload for Southend councillors led to calls for an increase in the number of councillors. A strong local campaign proved effective and in 2001 four new wards were created, making 17 wards and 51 councillors in total. The opportunity was taken to realign some ward boundaries – Shoebury in particular had grown out of all proportion since the last review.

Finally for the local authority, there were changes in Council structure, introduced following a government initiative to make councillors more professional and accountable. In January 2000 Southend introduced a new 'Cabinet' system, with eight executive councillors in charge of themed portfolios (environment, health, etc.) and three 'scrutiny committees' to check their every move. The system is likely to evolve over the first few years of operation.

## Unfulfilled Ambitions

Not all Southend's dreamed of schemes have been fulfilled.

In 1950 the Council noted the 'very considerable development' at Warners Bridge and suggested the construction of a railway station there to serve both the residents and the airport. Plans for this were reaffirmed by Regional Airports Limited in the mid-1990s, but it has still to materialise.

In 1951 there was talk of reclaiming the foreshore near the pier and building a marina. Numerous such schemes have since been proposed, the most recent by Brent Walker in 1986, complete with harbour, marine village, golf course, hotel and sports centre. It never happened. Since then, much of Southend's foreshore has been

**162**  The old gasworks site on Southend seafront, a prime site for development.

designated a nature reserve, so development looks unlikely.

In 1966 the Council considered introducing a hovercraft scheme, but nothing came of it. The Council's current transport strategy, however, includes the provision of a hovercraft terminal near the pier to capitalise on the under-utilised river, so maybe it will reach fruition this time?

There has been talk since the late 1960s of developing the abandoned gasworks site, but the toxic nature of the land has constantly been a barrier. This is a prime seafront site – ideal for a hotel or conference centre, backed up by shops and housing – but the money (and perhaps sufficient will-power) has not been forthcoming.

Inland there has been talk since the early 1970s of dualling Priory Crescent – the only non-dualled stretch of road between Bournes Green and London. However, Priory Park (and/or the mature trees outside it) would be adversely affected by any road-widening scheme and, as the Park was given as a recreational gift to the town 'in perpetuity' by R.A. Jones, there is a strong body of local opinion against any encroachment. More than 12,000 people signed a petition against

**163**  The new pierhead lifeboat station and sundeck under construction in June 2001.

road-widening for just that reason in 1974. The Council's current transport strategy lists Priory Crescent improvement as one of its key targets and battle lines are already being drawn.

Perhaps the biggest disappointment in unfulfilled ambitions is the pier. Since the 1976 pierhead fire, schemes for its redevelopment have come and gone, with little to show for them. Small improvements have been made – there's a temporary theatre there now, and a new lifeboat house and sundeck opened in 2001 – but what is really needed is large-scale redevelopment of the pier as a whole. There has been much talk of a themed Victorian- or Edwardian-style pier or a record-breaking pierhead rollercoaster, but neither seems anywhere near reality. Nevertheless, visitor numbers – 400,000 in 1999 – have at least been picking up in recent years.

**Southend Today**

Southend today is a thriving, bustling place: a regional shopping and employment centre with a rejuvenated seafront and buzzing nightlife. The 1990s has seen 'a new wave of optimism to capture the lost magic' and Southend can be proud and optimistic again.

The challenges for the future are many. Perhaps the biggest is to balance the provision of housing and facilities for a rising population with a growing environmental awareness. Penned in by Green Belt, the town has nowhere to go and the Council and developers are turning instead to the regeneration of derelict urban land. With several recent campaigns against development on the fringes of the borough, this has to be the right way. The sale of Shoebury Garrison (which closed in 1998) for housing and recreation is a good example of possible land reuse, and other Ministry of Defence land at the nearby New Ranges is destined to follow, but what will be the implications for traffic movement on this 'wrong' side of town?

Proposed development of land at Bournes Green was turned down by the government in the early 1970s and by the late 1980s the Council had recognised that 'greater public awareness of the environmental costs of new roads ... has resulted in the scaling down of some major road proposals in the borough'. The recent release of Green Belt land at Fossetts Farm for development has been full of controversy.

A controversial factor in recent population growth has been the enforced housing of refugees in the town. This has led to social problems, including violence. There is a clear balancing act to be managed.

Southend Council has launched a number of initiatives in the last few years to involve local townsfolk in making Southend a better place to live. A Quality of Life initiative, a Local Transport Plan and a Cultural Strategy have been instituted and there are plans for future Neighbourhood Forums. With money coming from Europe, the Lottery and the government (Southend has been included in the Thames Gateway regeneration area) the future looks bright.

Southend has expanded beyond all recognition since its humble origins as a fishing hamlet just 300 years ago and it has seen a lot of changes on the way, but it has not lost sight of its history and heritage. The *Royal Hotel*, the pier and the Kursaal all survive, as do streets of Victorian and Edwardian housing.

'The past,' wrote Southend author Warwick Deeping, 'is full of colour and passion and humour,' and we can learn from it some valuable lessons.

History may not be in your face in muchlamented Southend, but it is there. You have only to open your eyes to see it.

**164** The new 'town square' at Victoria Circus, showing the new (1996) *Odeon* cinema and the Millennium clock.

# Select Bibliography

The items listed below were extremely useful in the research for this book.

*A Guide to Southend by a Gentleman* (1824)

Archer, Thomas, *A Poetical Description of New Southend* (1794)

Benton, Philip, *The History of Rochford Hundred* (1867-88 [1991 reprint])

Brake, George Thompson, *Lessons from Licensing and Policing in a 20th Century Town* (1997)

Brake, George Thompson, *The Scene of Early Methodism in the Rochford Hundred* (1994)

Bride, H.N., *Old Leigh* (1967)

Bride, H.N., *The Story of Southend Pier* (undated, but *c.*1960s)

Bundock, John F., *Leigh Parish Church of St Clement* (1980)

Bundock, John F., *Old Leigh – A Pictorial History* (1978)

Burrows, J.W. and Jennings, George, *Porters – Description & History* (1934)

Burrows, J.W., *Southend-on-Sea & District* (1909 [1970 reprint])

Burrows, J.W., *The History of Prittlewell Priory* (1922 [rewritten and abridged by Leonard Helliwell in 1970])

Burrows, V.E., *The Tramways of Southend-on-Sea* (1965)

Carmichael, Harry, *With Future, With Past* (1995)

Crouch, Marcus, *Essex* (1969)

Crowe, Ken, *A History of Southend's Museums* (1994)

Crowe, Ken, *Britain in Old Photographs – Southend-on-Sea* (1995)

Crowe, Ken, *Southend Then & Now* (1984)

Dally, Keith, *St John the Baptist, Southend-on-Sea – A History* (1992)

Deeping, Warwick, *St John's Parish Church, Southend-on-Sea (Recollections)*, (1950)

Delahoy, Richard, *Southend Corporation Transport* (1986)

Department of the Environment, *List of Buildings of Special Architectural or Historical Interest – Southend-on-Sea* (1974)

Dilley, Roy, *The Dream Palaces of Southend* (1983)

Dow, George, *LTS Album* (1981)

Dowie, Peggy and Crowe, Ken, *A Century of Iron* (1989)

Dowie, Peggy and Crowe, Ken, *The Longest Pier in the World* (1986)

Essex Record Office, *Essex at War 1939-45* (1995)

Everritt, Sylvia, *Southend Seaside Holiday* (1980)

Feather, Fred, *The Borough Men* (1992)

Frost, K.A. and Carson, D.J., *Southend Pier Railway* (1990)

Gayner, Arthur J., *Almost a Century – The Story of Southend-on-Sea Fire Brigade* (1993)

Gifford & Partners, *Old Ranges, Shoeburyness, Essex – An Archaeological and Historic Building Assessment (Vols I & II)* (1997)

Gifford & Partners, *Report on an Archaeological Evaluation at The Old Ranges, Shoeburyness, Essex (Vols I & II)* (1999)

Glennie, Donald, *Our Town* (1947)

Goodale, Alfred P., *Southchurch – A Short History* (1995)

Goody, Dave and Miles, Peter, *Potted Shrimps – Southend United Encyclopaedia* (1999)

Gowing, Ellis N., *The Story of Prittlewell Church* (1958)

Granville, Dr. A.B., *Spas of England* (1841 [1971 edition])

Helliwell, Leonard, *Prittlewell Priory* (1980 [second edition, reprint])

Helliwell, Leonard, *South East Essex in the Saxon Period* (1971)

Helliwell, Leonard, *Southchurch Hall – An Illustrated Guide* (1969)

Herbert, A.P., *The War Story of Southend Pier* (1945)

Hill, Tony, *Guns & Gunners at Shoeburyness* (1999)

Hodgkins, John R., *The History of Cliff Town Congregational Church, Southend-on-Sea, 1799-1972* (1974)

Hollander, D. (ed.), *The History of Southend Airport* (1998)

Hunt, Leslie, *Bleriot to BAE146 – The History of Southend Airport 1915-93* (1993)

Jefferies, Malcolm and Lee, J. Alfred, *The Hospitals of Southend* (1986)

*John H. Burrows, 1854-1935 – A Memoir* (1935)

Kay, Peter, *The London, Tilbury & Southend Railway* (both volumes) (1996 and 1997)

*Kelly's Directory* (various)

King, Tom and Furbank, Kevan, *The Southend Story* (1991)

Knill, Victor, *The Island Church – St Augustine of Canterbury, Thorpe Bay* (1997)

MacLeod, Donald G., *South East Essex in the Prehistoric Period* (1971)

Martin, Chris, *Shoeburyness* (1982)

Mason, Peter and Goody, David, *Southend United – The Official History of the 'Blues'* (1993)

Mee, Arthur, *The King's England – Essex* (1942)

Melling, John Kennedy, *Southend Playhouses from 1793* (1969)

Morant, Philip, *The History & Antiquities of the County of Essex* (1768 [1978 reprint])

*Order of Service and Procedure at the Commemoration of the Centenary of the Birth of the late Robert Arthur Jones MBE*

Orford, Maureen, *The Shoebury Story* (2000)

Payne, Jessie K., *Southend-on-Sea – A Pictorial History* (1985)

Pevsner, Nikolaus, *The Buildings of England – Essex* (1988 [reprint])

Pewsey, Stephen, *The Book of Southend-on-Sea* (1993)

Phillips, Charles, *The Shenfield to Southend Line* (1984)

Pitt-Stanley, Sheila, *Legends of Leigh* (1989)

Pollitt, William, *A History of Prittlewell* (1951)

Pollitt, William, *Southchurch and its Past* (1949)

Pollitt, William, *The Rise of Southend* (1957)

*Post Office Directory* (1874)

*Prittlewell Parish Vestry Minutes* (1624 onwards)

Rodwell, Warwick, *South East Essex in the Roman Period* (1971)

*Royal Commission on Historic Monuments (Volume IV – South East Essex)* (1923)

Searle, Muriel V., *Down the Line to Southend* (1984)

Shepherd, E.W., *The Story of Southend Pier* (1979)

Sherringham, Denis, *Growing up in Southend-on-Sea 1929-47* (1995)

Simpson, F.D. and Clark, P.F., *The Bridge Family & Its Buses* (1983)

Smith, J.R., *Edwardian Heyday* (1988)

Smith, J.R., *Southend Past* (1984 [reprint])

Smith, J.R., *The Origins and Failure of New South-End* (1991)

Snell, Peter J., *Westcliff-on-Sea Motor Services Ltd.* (1987)

Southend Local Board, *Minutes of* (1866–92)

Southend Society, *Southend's Heritage – Georgian and Victorian Terraces* (1983)

Southend-on-Sea Borough Council, *Minutes of* (1892–2001)

Southend-on-Sea Borough Council, *Population Estimates* (1998)

Spooner, B.M. and Bowdrey, J.P. (ed.), *Hadleigh Great Wood* (1988)

Stibbards, Phyl, *Our Past Has A Future – The Listed Buildings Of The Shoebury Area* (1988)

*Transactions of the Southend-on-Sea & District Antiquarian and Historical Society* (1921-51)

Victoria County History

Walker, Wendy, *Essex Markets & Fairs* (1981)

White, William, *Directory of Essex* (1848)

Woodgate, John, *The Essex Police* (1985)

Worsdale, Jim, *Southend at War* (1998)

Wright, Thomas, *The History of the County of Essex* (1831)

Wymer, J.J. and Brown, N.R., *North Shoebury: Settlement & Economy in South-east Essex, 1500BC-1500AD* (1995)

Yearsley, Ian, *Essex Events* (1999)

Yearsley, Ian, *Hadleigh Past* (1998)

Guidebooks to the following churches: Clifftown Congregational (Southend); Holy Trinity (Southchurch); St Augustine of Canterbury (Thorpe Bay); St Clement (Leigh); St John the Baptist (Southend); St Laurence & All Saints (Eastwood); and St Mary the Virgin (Prittlewell).

Various guides and booklets about Prittlewell Priory, Southchurch Hall, Porters and other selected heritage buildings in the borough, plus Scheduled Ancient Monument listings from the Department of Culture, Media & Sport and documentary information held in Southend's museums, such as the *Guided Walks* series and accompanying leaflets. Also, the Leigh Society leaflets *A Walk Through Old Leigh* and *A Walk Round Leigh Hill* and various Southend Borough Council publicity and town planning brochures, especially from the 1960s-2001.

Various issues of the following magazines and newspapers – *Essex Chronicle, Essex Countryside, Essex Past & Present, Evening Echo, Gentleman's Magazine, Leigh Times, Southend & Westcliff Graphic, Southend Standard, Southend Times* and *Yellow Advertiser*. Also, the Council's *Civic News* publication and the Leigh Society's newsletter, *Leighway*.

Videos – *By Its Dome It's Known, Southend Memories I, Southend Memories II* and *The Life & Times of Southend Pier*.

Southend's museums held many treasures of value and the Eastwood Millennium Project's 'Eastwood' exhibition helped my understanding of that parish's history.

Maps from all periods were indispensable.

# Index

References which relate to illustrations only are given in **bold**.

Absalom family, 93
Alexandra Road, 40
Alexandra Street, **39**, 40, 43, 45, 65, 86, 122
Alexandra Yacht Club, 50
All Saints Church, 41
Ambleside Drive, 69
*Angel*, 101
Archer Avenue, 115
Archer, Rev. Thomas, 26, 29, 51
Arnold, Thomas, 23
Arthur's Land, 23
Ash Walk, 23
Audley, Sir Thomas, 14
Austen, Jane, 29
Avenue Road, 16, **36**, 40
Aviation Way, 118

Balmoral Road, 67, 125
Bankside, 122-3
Bannester, Elizabeth, 74
Barking, 46, 55
Baxter Avenue, 79, 122
Baxter, J.G., 40, 51, 66
Bayeux, Bishop of, 99
Beecroft Art Gallery, 113
Belfairs, 80, **81**, 104-5, 113, 115
Benfleet, 35, 104
Benfleet, Battle of, 4
Benton, Philip, 8, 12, 15-16, 38, 41, 46, 49, 73, 101
Billericay, 14
Blakeman, Jeremiah, 26
Blenheim Chase, **84**, 85, 115
*Blue Boar*, 10, 12, 20, 46, 61, 65, 85
Bolingbroke, Viscount, 18
Boston Avenue, 70
Bournemouth Park Road, 70
Bournes Green, 2, 4, **61**, 62, 85, 102, 115, 140-1
Bournes Green Chase, 101, 133
Bow Window House, 27
Bradley, William, 50
Bradwell, 7
Brentwood, 35
Brewery Road, 45, 61, 69, 115
Brickhouse Farm, 115, 120
Bridge family, 91
Bridgewater Drive, 103
Brightwell, John Rumbelow, 52, 72, 95, 127

*Britannia*, 24, 42, 54, 67
Broadbridge, Lord, 111-2
Broadway (Leigh-on-Sea), **76**, 77
Broadway Market, 79
Bronze Age, 1-3, 66
Brook Road, 85
Brooke, Lady, 47
Browne, Humphrey, 19
Brunlees, Sir James, 49
Bryant Avenue, 62
Buchanan, Robert, 73
Bunyan, John, 99
Burges, Col. Y.H., 74
Burrows, John H., 50, 52, 73
Burrows, John.W., 37, 73, 89
buses, 90-1, 115, 125, 127
business, 72, 95-7, 114, 125-8, 131-6
Byrne Drive, 103

Carlton Bakery, **20**, 21
Cambridge Road, 41, **42**
Campbell Road, **107**, 125
Canvey Island, 5, 13
Capel Terrace, 37
Cardigan Avenue, **84**
Carlingford Drive, 82
Carlton Avenue, 82
Carnarvon Road, 122
Carnegie, Andrew, 70
Caroline Baths, 27-8, **43**
Case, Rev. Thomas, 20
Cashiobury Terrace, 37
*Castle*, **43**, 87
Castle Terrace, 87
Caulfield Road, 102
Chalkwell, 35, 45, 54, **56**, 57, 74, 77, 80, 92, 118
Chalkwell Avenue, 57
Chalkwell Esplanade, 57
Chalkwell Hall, 17-8, 57, 85
Chalkwell Park, 17, 69, **75**, 105, 113
Chalkwell Park Drive, 12, 58
Channon, Henry/Paul, 115
Chapman and André, **13**, 16-7, **23**
Chelmsford, 34, 98
Chelmsford Avenue, 51, 72
Cherry Orchard Lane/Way, 134-6
Chichester Road, **123**, 125, 127
Child, Sir Richard, 18
Church Road (Shoeburyness), **100**

Church Road (Southend), 131
Churchill Gardens, 122
cinemas, 65, 94, **96**, 131, 139, **141**
Civic Centre, 119-22
Civil War, 19
Clarence Road, 51, 69, 119
Clarence Street, 27, 30, 37, 45
cliff lift, 54
Cliff Town, **36**, 37-40, **43**, 45, 123, 130-1
Cliffs Pavilion, 113, 137
Clifftown Congregational Church, 37, **38**, 51
Clifftown Parade, 52, 54, 63
Clifftown Road, **37**, 45
Clifton Terrace, **54**
Colchester, 35, 48
Coleman Street, 41
Constable, John, 29, 77
Constable Way, 115
Corsham Road, 122
Cotgrove's, 72
courthouse, 43
*Cricketers*, 40, 61, 67
Crowstone Road, **56**, 72
Crowstone, the, 17, **57**
Cuckoo Corner, **84**, 85, 102, 122

Danes, 4
Darnley Road, 122
Davies, Mary, 9
de Essex, Robert, 9
de Southchurch family, 15, 59
Deeds Cottage, **20**, 21
Deeping, Dr. George, 73
Deeping, Warwick, 73, 127, 141
Dent, Rev. Arthur, 99
Denys, Lady Charlotte, 27, 29
Disraeli, Benjamin, **18**, 30
Dixon's, 97, **126**, 127
Domesday Book, 9, 14, 16, 60, 76, 99
Dowsett Avenue, 52, 122
Dowsett, Thomas, 40, 51-2, 66, 72, 89
*Duchess of York*, 25-6
*Duke of Clarence*, 25, 27
Dulverton Avenue, **82**
Durer, Albrecht, 9

Eagle Way, 115
Earls Hall, 14-15, 18, **34**, 82, 87, 102

Earls Hall Avenue, 15, 102, **103**
Earls Hall School, 15
East Street (Leigh-on-Sea), 82
East Street (Prittlewell), 10, **11**, 12, 14, 19,
  **20**, 22, **34**, 38, 42, 46, 48, 69
Eastern Avenue, 3, 13, **68**, **83**, 85, 113,
  115, 134, 136
Eastern Esplanade, **44**, **52**, 54, **57**, 69, 87,
  89, **106**, 113, 137
Eastwood, 7, 10, 13, 30, 75-7, 80, 85, 91,
  98-9, 102-3, 105, 114-15, 133-4, 136
Eastwood Boulevard/Lane, 85, 90
Eastwood church, 99, 119, **135**
Eastwood Rise, 91
Eastwood Road, 80, **81**
Eastwood Road North, 102
Eastwoodbury Lane, 99, 104, 134
education, 10, 14, 20, 42-3, 68-70, 87, 115
Edwards Hall/Park, 91
Edwards Hall Motors, 91
EKCO, 97, 107, 114
electoral representation, 45, 51, 53, 74-7,
  115, 120, 128-9, 139
Elizabeth I, 19
Elizabeth II, **112**, 123, 139
Elm Road (Leigh-on-Sea), 97
Elm Road (Shoeburyness), 100
Elmer Approach, 127
entertainment, 28, 63-6, 92-5, 111-13, 129,
  136-9
Eton House School, 29
Evans, Sir David, 50

Fairfax Drive, **56**, 82, 115
Fairway, The, 115
*Falcon*, 30
Farringdon Place/Service Road, 127
fire brigade, **44**, 45, 67, 76-7, 97, 103, 105,
  115, 120, 122, 128-9
First World War, 54, 65, 74, 78-80, 86-7,
  89, 93, 97, 105, 136
Fitzwimarc, Robert, 99
Fossetts Farm, 2-3, 141
Foulness Island, 5
Fox Hall Farmhouse, **101**, 102, **138**, 139
Francis, Sir John, 87
Francis, Joseph, 52, 80

Gainsborough Drive, 82
Garon family, 67, 72, 95, 97
Garon Leisure Park, 138-9
Gas, Light & Coke Company, 87, 103, 114
gasworks, 2, 41, 58, 80, 87, 140
George IV, 29
George V, 93
George VI, 80, 87
*Golden Lion*, 20
Gosset, Daniel Wright, 52
Grand Drive, 12-3, 58
*Grand Hotel* (Southend), 25-8
Grand Terrace, 25-6, **28**, 29
Grainger Road, 95, 114
Granville, Dr. A.B., 32
Great Wakering, 5, 61, 102
Gregson, William, 39, 46, 50, 52, 72
Greyhound Retail Park, 95, 133
Grove House, 26-7

Grove Road, 27, 131
Grove Terrace, 25, 33, 45, 65, 94
Grover Street, 125

Hadleigh, 22, 61, 75, 85, 98, 104
*Halfway House*, **54**, 62
Hall Road, 134
Hamilton, Lady, 29
Hamlet Court, 16
Hamlet Court Road, 16-7, 45, 55, 72, 86
Hamlet Farm, 15
Hamlet Road, 38, 40
Hammerson development, **126**, 127-8, 131
Hampton Gardens, 103
Hamstel Road, 13, 82, 85, 90, 115
Hare, H.T., 69-70
Hastings Road, 4
Hawkwell, 99
Hawtree, Supt. Samuel, 43
Henry VIII, 10
Heygate, Anna, **39**
Heygate, Miss E.A., 41
Heygate, James (junior), 39, 41
Heygate, James (senior), 26, 30, 39
Heygate, Sir William, 30-1, 39
High Street (Leigh-on-Sea), 76-7, 92, 115,
  118
High Street (Shoeburyness), 99, 115
High Street (Southend), 25-7, **29**, 30, 33,
  37, 40, 42-3, 45-6, 61, 69, 72, 86-7,
  90, 94, **96**, **108**, 115, 122-3, 125, **126**,
  127, 131, 136
Highfield Crescent, 82
Highlands Boulevard, 85
Holland, Thomas, 26
*Hope Hotel*, 24, 26-7
*Horse & Groom*, 99
hospitals, 46-7, 51, 67, 97, 115, 125, **135**,
  136
*Hotel Victoria*, 72, 97, 127
hotels, 72

Ingram, James Colbert, 51-2, 66
Iron Age, 1, 4
Iveagh, Earl of, 97-8, 115

Jenkins, Sir Brian, 136
Jerrold, Samuel, 29
Jesus Guild, 8, 10, 20
Jones, Edward Cecil, 87, 97, 113-5
Jones Memorial Ground, **83**, 87, 113
Jones, Robert Arthur ('R.A.'), 72, 87-8,
  95, **108**, 140

Keddie's, 72, 125, 131, 136
Kenilworth Gardens, **84**, 85, 115
Kent Elms, **105**
Kerslake, H.M., **80**
*King's Head*, 20
Knights Hospitaller, 18
Knights Templar, 18
Kursaal, 12, 22, 66-7, 92-5, 111-12, 130,
  137-8, 141

Langham, Lady, 29
Leas, The, **53**
Leigh Hall Road, 77

Leigh Road, 17, 69, **75**
Leigh-on-Sea, 2, 4, 6-7, 12, 16-7, 30, 35,
  53, 58, 61, 73, 75-7, 79-80, **81**, 82,
  85, 91-2, 97-9, 103, 106, 115-18, 139
Leyland, Constance, 86, 120
libraries, 27, 29, 70, **71**, **86**, 89, **119**, 120,
  **121**, 122, 139
lifeboats, 50, 94, 106, **140**, 141
Lifstan Way, 58, 85
Lillingston, Rev. George, 33
Lingwood, Capt. G., 45
London, 12, 18-19, 25-30, 32, 35-7, 48,
  80, 93, 95, 103, 105-6, 114, 140
London, Bishop of, 33
London, Lord Mayor of, 18, 30-1, 50, 80,
  112, 136
London Road, 13, 15, **16**, 25, **29**, 30, **33**,
  40, 43, 45-6, 52, **56**, 61, 65, 69, 77,
  79-80, 86, 89, 115, 122, 127, 131, **132**,
  133
*London Tavern*, 45
Luker, Henry, 45
Luker Road, 45
Luker's Brewery, 45, 94
Lutyens, Sir Edwin, 80

MacDonald Avenue, 70
Manners Way, **84**, 103
Maplin Airport, 119
Maplin Way, 115
Marine Parade (Southend), 23, **27**, **52**, 54,
  63, 92, **94**, 112
Market Place, 45
Market Road, 26-7
Martin, Albert, 89, 97
Mary, Queen, 19
Mason, George, 17
Mayfield Avenue, 102, **103**
Methodist Church, **44**
Middlesex Avenue, 82
Middleton Brewery, 45
*Middleton Hotel*, 45, 61
Miles, William, 114
Milton, 7, 10, 12-13, 15-17, 21, 25, 30,
  32, 34, **36**, 37, 40, **43**, 45, 55, 57-8,
  74, 76, 134
Milton Hall, 15-16, 24, 41, 48
Milton Place, 38, 40
Milton Road, 12, 16-17, 38, 41, **42**, 45
Milton Street, 41, 48, 125
*Minerva*, 24, 28, 30, 38, 50, 54, 58, 61-2,
  66

Nazareth House, 15, **16**, 41
Neave, Sir Arundell, 9, 15
Nelson Street (Terrace), 37, 45
Nestuda Way, **135**, 136
Never Never Land, 93, 137
Newington Avenue, 115
Nicholson, Sir Charles, 19, 89
Nolan, Rev. Frederick, 34
Norden, John, 13, 19
Nore, the, 26, 106
North Road (Prittlewell), 12, 15, 17, **47**,
  48, 61, 67
North Shoebury, 1, 4, 6-7, 10, 98-102,
  115, 133-4

North Shoebury church, 100, **101**, 133
North Shoebury Road, 99, 101, 133
North Street (Prittlewell), 10, **11**, 12, 14, 19-20, **21**, **34**, 38, 46
Northumberland Avenue, **114**
Nottingham, Earl of, 14-16

Oaken Grange Drive, 103
Odeon cinema, 45
office blocks, 122, **128**, 131-3
Old Southend Lane/Road, 12, 22, **24**, **33**, 45
Outing Close, 22
Oxford, Earls of, 15
oysters, 22-3, 30

Pall Mall, 77
*Palace Hotel*, 72, **73**, 79-80, 94, 106
*Palmeira Towers*, 129
Park Crescent, 40
Park Estate, 40, 45
Park Road, 16, 38, 40
Park Street, 122-3, **124**
*Park Tavern*, 40
Park Terrace, 40
Parkanaur Avenue, 74
*Parsons Barn*, 101, **134**
Peasants' Revolt, 19, 60
Peck, Rev. Samuel, 19
Peck, Rev. Thomas, 19
pedestrianisation, 125-7, 131
*Peter Boat*, 76
Peter Pan's Playground, 94, 115, 138
Peto, Brassey and Betts, 36
Peveral, Ranulf, 76
Pevsner, Sir Nikolaus, 69
Pier Hill, 23, **24**, **27**, **28**, 29, **31**, 49, 63, **64**, **73**, 93, 112, 131, 136
*Pier Hotel*, 45
Pitsea, 46, 55
plague, 19
Pleasant Row, 23, 45
*Plough*, **65**
police, 43, 75, 77, **80**, 97, 103, **119**, 120, 122, 128-9
Pollitt, William, 89
population figures, 32, 57, 77, 82, 100, 103, 111, 134, 141
Port of London Authority, 18
Porters (Grange), 18-19, 30, 41, 45, **51**, 58, 89, 122-3
Porters Grange Avenue, 122
Porters Town, 41, **43**, 45, 123
Post Office, 30, 46, 133
Poynters Lane, 101
Pratt, Watts & Lowdoun, 25-6
Prevost, Alfred, 52
Prince Avenue, 82
Prince George, 93, **95**
Prince Henry, 82
Princes Street, **40**
Princess Anne, 125, 131
Princess Caroline, **28**, 29
Princess Charlotte, 29
Priors Hall, 14-16, 20-2, 24, **34**, 40
Priory Crescent, 4-5, **12**, **83-4**, 85, 97, 140-1
Priory Park, 4, 7, 10, 12, **14-15**, 18, **83-4**,

85, 87, **88**, 137, 140
Prittle Brook, 4, 9, **56**, 80, **81**, 82, 105
Prittlewell, **5**, 7-23, 26, 29-30, 32-4, 37-9, 42-3, 45-8, 51, 53, 57-8, 60-1, 65, 69, 73-4, 77, 80, 85-6, 99, 122, 130
Prittlewell Chase, **56**, **84**, 85, 87, 97, 115, 139
Prittlewell church, 4, 6-10, **11**, 14-15, 20, **36**, 38, 47-8, 67, 122
Prittlewell Church School, 20, 34, 69-70
Prittlewell fair, 13, 19-20
Prittlewell lock-up, 19
Prittlewell market, 13
Prittlewell Parish Burial Ground, 47-8, 67-8
Prittlewell Priory, **8**, 9-10, 41, 87, 89
Prittlewell School Board, 42
Prittlewell workhouse, 19-20, **88**
Progress Road, 114
Prospect Place/Row, 113
Public Hall, **39**, 40, 43, 65
Purchas, Rev. Samuel, 99

Quebec Avenue, **91**
Queen Mother, 98, 120, **121**
Queens Road, **40**, 45
Queensway, 13, 18, 123

*Railway Tavern*, 37
railways, 4, 17, 34-7, 45-6, 48, 55, **57**, **63**, 77, **83**, 91-2, **96**, 101, 106, 115, 122-3, 125, 139
Ramuz Drive, **56**
Ramuz, Frederick Francis, 52, 77
Rasch, Major and Mrs. Carne, 47, 52
Rayleigh, 13, 98-9
Rayleigh House, 30
Rayleigh Road, 99, 102, 115
Reay, Rev. Thomas Osmotherley, 48
Recreation Avenue, 58
Reid, Sir C. Hercules, 87
religion, 30, 37-8, 70-2
Remnant, John, 23
Reynolds, 21
Rich, Lord Richard, 14-16, 18, 60, 76, 99
Ring Road, 122-5, **126**, 127, 130-1
River Roach, 2, 99
River Thames, 1, 5, **17**, 18, 32, 78-9, 106-7
river transport, 30, 35-6, 63, 112, 140
Road to the West, 118
Rochford, 12-13, 19, 25, 30, **34**, 59-61, 99, 103, 105
Rochford Hall, 14, 18
Rochford Road, 12-3
Romans, 4-5
Roots Hall, 4
Royal Artillery Way, 3
Royal Hill, **28**, 29, 31, 49
*Royal Hotel*, **24-5**, 30, **31**, 40, 130-1, 141
Royal Terrace, **28**, 29, 35-7, 40, 93, 106
Royals, The, 131, **132**
Ruskin Avenue, 67, **68**, 82

Sadd, Rev. Arthur, 72
St Bernard's School, **42**
St Erkenwald's Church, 70-2

St John the Baptist Church, 33, 38-9, 42, 45, 47, 52, 68, 70, 72-3
Salisbury Avenue, **107**
Sanderson, John, 26
Saxons, 5-7
Scratton, Daniel, 14, 16, 20, 25
Scratton, Daniel Robert, 14, 40
Scratton, John Bayntun, 30
Scratton Road, 14
Sea Life Centre, 27, **43**, 137, **138**
Seaway, 112, 122
Second World War, 105-10, 113
sewage works, 53, **83-4**
Shenfield, 48
*Ship* (Leigh-on-Sea), 118
*Ship Hotel* (Southend), 23, 25-7, 30
Shoeburyness, 1-2, 4-5, 22, 31, 46, 61-2, 82, 99-100, 102-3, 106, 115, 119, 139
Shoebury Garrison, 4-5, 46, 90, 99-100, 107, 141
Shopland, 13, **101**, 102, 139
Shorefields, 25, 113
Shrubbery, The, 30, 49, 93
South End, 21-34, 130
South Shoebury, 7, 46, 98-101, 103
South Shoebury church, 99
Southbourne Grove, 79, **81**, 82
Southchurch, 1-2, 7, 12-13, 16, 21-2, 29, 45-6, 58-62, 66, 68, 73-4, 76-7, 79, 82, 85, 91, 99, 115
Southchurch Avenue, 12, 22, 61-2, 72
Southchurch Boulevard, 62, **102**, 115
Southchurch church, 29
Southchurch Hall, 13, 19, 59-60, 89
Southchurch Lawn, 29
Southchurch National School, 58, 69, 115
Southchurch Park, 66, 89, 105, 115
Southchurch Road, 12, 22, 41, 46, 58, 62, 115, **116**, 127
Southchurch Wick, 60
Southend District Antiquarian & Historical Society, 89
*Southend & Westcliff Graphic*, 79
Southend Airport, 104-5, 107, 118-9, 136, 139
Southend Airshow, 136, **137**
Southend Arterial Road (A127), 82, 103, 114, 134, **135**
Southend Carnival, 97-8, 112
Southend Central Museum, 5, 21, 70, **119**, **121**, 122
Southend Central Station, 35, 48, 92, 115
Southend Gas Company, 41, 53, 87
Southend High School, 70, 87, 115
Southend Institute, 51, 68
Southend Lane, 12, 22-3
Southend Local Board, 16, 38-41, 43, 45-6, 48-51, 54-5
Southend National School, 42, **44**, 69, 87
Southend Park, 40
Southend Pier, **frontispiece**, 30-3, 36, 48-50, 63, 65, **66**, 93-4, **95**, 105-6, 111-13, 130-1, **138**, **140**, 141
Southend Society, 130
*Southend Standard*, 46, 48, 50, 73
Southend Town Council, 50-77
Southend United, 3, 65, 94-5, 114, 139

Southend Victoria Station, 48, 92, 115, **124**, 127, 133
Sparrow, Lady Olivia, 77
*Spread Eagle*, 20, 34
Springfield Drive, 82
Stoker's Lane, **68**
Stone Age, 1
*Strawberry Field*, 134
Strutt, General William Goodday, 30
Strutt's Parade, 30
Sutherland Boulevard, 85
Sutton, 10, 13, 18
Sutton Road, 12, 19, 22, **34**, 41, 67-8, 82, 85, **88**, 120, 123
Sutton Street, 41
Sweyn, 9, 14, 99
Sykes, Sir Francis, 30

Talza Arcade, 127
Tabor, James, 18
Technical College, 69-70, 72, 87, 97, 122, **126-8**, 131, 139
Temple Farm, 4, 13
Temple Farm Industrial Estate, 18
Temple Sutton, 18
Thames Farm, 23, 45
theatre, 28-30, 65
Thomas, Rev. John, 19
Thompson, Sir William, 31
Thorpe Bay, 1, 73-4, 77, 82, 85, 92, 100, 102, 105, 107, 115
Thorpe Hall, 1, 6, 60, **61**, 62, 74
Thorpe Hall Avenue/Lane, 62, **63**, 74, **102**
Thundersley, 98
Thurlow-Baker, R.H., 98
Tilbury, 7, 35-6, 46
tithe maps, **33-4**

Tolhurst, Bernard Wilshire, 52, 66
Tompkins, Herbert, 89
trolley buses, 90-1
Trotter, Thomas, 28, 65
trams, **44**, 60-3, 76-7, 89-91, 105
Tudor Road, 91
Two Tree Island, 115
Tylers Avenue, 65, 67, 97, 120, 133
Tyrone Road, 74
Tyrrell family, 17, 19

Underhill, Rev. Edward, 19-20

Vandervoord family, 24, 30
Vassal, John, 99
Victoria Arcade, 97, 127
Victoria Avenue, 10, **11**, 14, **15**, 20-1, **34**, **43**, 46, 48, 52, 70, **71**, 79, 85, **86**, 87, **119**, 120, **121**, 122, 127, 139
Victoria Circus, 46, 61, 69, 72, 79, 86-7, 91, 97, 115, 122, 125, 127-8, **141**
Victoria Plaza, 127, 139
Victoria, Queen, 46, **47**, 50, 52
Victory Path, 80
Victory Sports Ground, 87, **88**

Wakering Road, 100
Wales, Prince of, 50
Wanstead, 18
war: Boer, 65; with France, 76; with Holland, 19, 76; with Spain, 76 (*See* First World War and Second World War under separate entries.)
Warners Bridge, 13, 99, 104, 136, 139
Warrior Square, 45-6, **47**, 90, 94, 97, 113, 115, 125, 139
Warwick, Dr., 46, 73

Warwick, Earls of, 14, 16, 76, 99
waterworks, 41, **42**, 45, 53
Wellington, Duke of, 18
Wesley, John, 77
West Road (Prittlewell), 12, 17, **55**, **65**, 79
West Road (Shoeburyness), 99
West Street (Leigh-on-Sea), 6
West Street (Prittlewell), 10, 12, 17, 19, 21, **34**, 46, 61, 65
Westborough Road, **55**
Westbourne Grove, 82
Westcliff Esplanade, 129
Westcliff High School, 12, **85**, 87
Westcliff Leisure Centre, 93, 113
Westcliff Swimming Baths, 93, 113
Westcliff-on-Sea, 17, 45, 54-6, 65, 67, 74, 77, 79, 107
Westcliff-on-Sea Motor Services Ltd., 91
Western Approaches, 133
Western Esplanade, 49, **52-3**, 54, **57**, 87, 93
*White Horse*, 58, **59**, 62
White House Road, 99
Whitegate Road, 45, 125
Whitwell, Mrs., 79
Wickford, 48
Wigram, Rev. Spencer, 42, 48
Wilson, Sir Thomas, 30
windmills, 16, 20, **36**
Woodgrange Drive, 45, 122
Wright, Edward, 52
Wright, Thomas, 30

York, Duke of, 87, **88**
York Road (formerly York Street), 26, 45, 70, **71**, 125